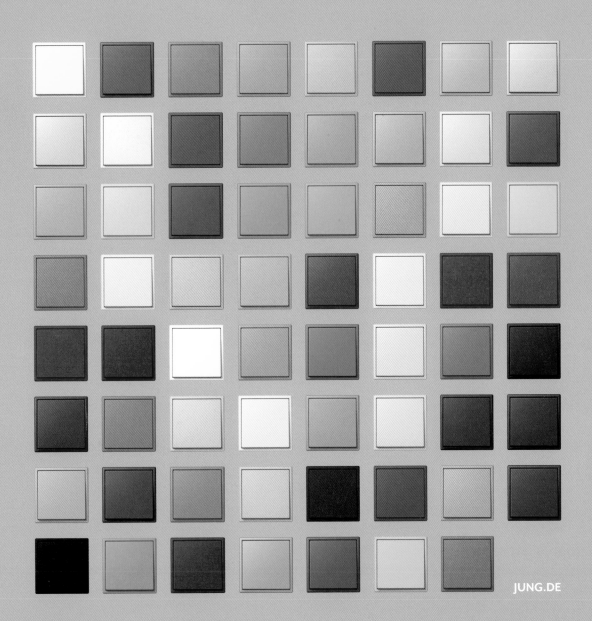

JUNG.DE

Out NOW

**JO NAGASAKA /
Schemata Architects**

Jo Nagasaka's focus is often drawn to tired, found objects or unused spaces. Through investigations to seek modern solutions and pioneering re-purposing techniques, he manages to transform interiors and breathe life back into objects. This book encapsulates the essence of the studio's work. **€39**

Jo Nagasaka /
Schemata Architects

Jo Nagasaka /
Schemata Architects

The evolution of Jo Nagasaka
a unique publication a
ry of Schemata A
dio's work
es

HAPPENING 2
Design for Events

Happening 2 journeys into the world of event design, vibrantly showcasing over 60 stunning spectacles – from fashion shows to festivals and exhibitions to exclusive product launches – that leave lasting impressions. **€69**

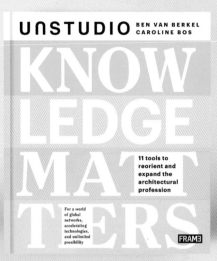

KNOWLEDGE MATTERS
UNStudio

The changing role of the architect has led to a reorganisation of UNStudio's practice and the introduction of Knowledge Platforms. Now compiled into an inspiring publication, *Knowledge Matters* explains this development and presents numerous examples of application. **€29**

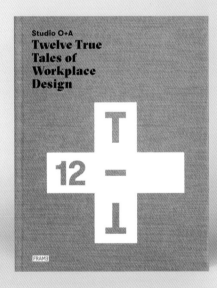

STUDIO O+A
Twelve True Tales of Workplace Design

This artfully-designed book tells Studio O+A's design story in a series of twelve true tales – plus a bonus comic book in the middle of it all – that accentuate the company's spirit of innovation. **€39**

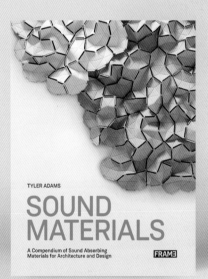

SOUND MATERIALS
A Compendium of Sound Absorbing Materials for Architecture and Design

Navigating the field of sound absorbing materials, this definitive resource guide provides context, examples, inspiration and direction to help users explore the 100+ materials presented for specific acoustic applications. **€29**

Order at FRAME.SHOP

FRAME

Check out *Mark's* new website

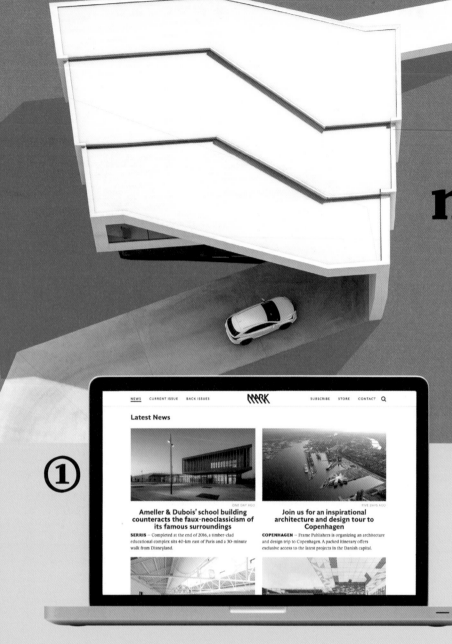

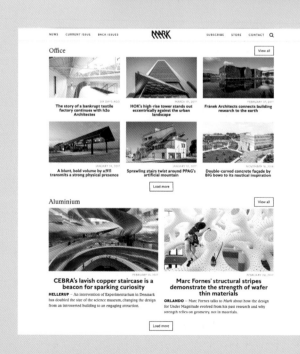

1 Latest News
This section brings you short reviews of buildings that have caught our attention.

2 Tags
Browse through online articles about specific architects, or buildings sharing specific characteristics, by using our tags.

3 Back Issues
Do you like the current issue and wonder what we have published before? See detailed information about previous issues.

4 Search Back Issues
Looking for print articles about a specific architect, building type, city or country? Our index has all the information!

5 About
Want to learn more about *Mark*? Look here for a concise history of the magazine.

mark-magazine.com

Plan

044

010   **Notice Board**

020   **Cross Section**

022   **Extrastudio** Vendas de Azeitão
024   **Salottobuono** Mexico City
026   **Ryu Mitarai** Tokyo
028   **Elding Oscarson** Lund
030   **Production Design**
032   **Christ & Gantenbein** Pratteln
034   **Rosenbaum and Aleph Zero** Formoso do Araguaia
036   **Marieke Kums and Junya Ishigami** Tytsjerk
038   **Infographic**
040   **Terra e Tuma** São Paulo
042   **Chance de Silva** London
044   **Ram Arkitektur** Espedalen
046   **Suppose Design Office** Tokoname
048   **Studio MK27** Catuçaba
050   **Dollhouses**

Ram Arkitektur
Log tower in Espedalen
Photo Sam Hughes

052   **Perspective Beirut**

054   **Stephanie Akkaoui Hughes** discusses citizens' rights to their city.
056   **Bernard Khoury** no longer responds to future urban plans for the Lebanese capital.
068   **Herzog & de Meuron**'s Beirut Terraces project suggests transparency, but it is first of all an accumulation of single luxury apartments.
076   **Youssef Tohme**'s architecture is defined by Lebanon's political structure and its rugged geography.

056

Bernard Khoury
Apartment building in Beirut
Photo Ieva Saudargaite

088   <u>Long Section</u>

090   **C.F. Møller**'s Copenhagen International School is a pioneer in an industrial-transformation zone.

100   **Bureau Spectacular**'s projects are getting bigger and more concrete, without sacrificing a sense of humour.

110   **Office KGDVS**'s Solo House exemplifies an ongoing shift towards exceptionality in contemporary architecture.

120   **Thomas Kröger** creates something new out of what we think we know.

136   **Giancarlo Mazzanti** provided a kindergarten in Barranquilla with a stimulating environment.

146   Three works of art by **Doug Aitken** consider modern life through modern architecture.

154   **Aires Mateus** built a Faculty of Architecture that allows freedom of appropriation.

162   **Mark Cousins** has spent half a life lecturing at the Architectural Association.

166   <u>Tools</u>

176   <u>Exit</u>

100

Bureau Spectacular
Another Primitive Hut in Los Angeles
Photo Injee Unshin

120

Thomas Kröger
House in Pinnow
Photo Thomas Heimann

CUSTOM MADE COLORS

Creativity, Passion, Customization

ENIGMA: The new gastronomic space of Albert Adrià designed by RCR Arquitectes (Pritzker Prize 2017) and Pau Llimona
where NEOLITH recreates a dreamlike landscape with a unique design, applied in claddings, countertops and flooring of the entire restaurant.

Discover all the design possibilities and the extraordinary features offered by NEOLITH at www.neolith.com

Mark is published
6 times a year by

Frame Publishers
Laan der Hesperiden 68
1076 DX Amsterdam
T +31 20 330 0630
F +31 20 428 0653
mark@frameweb.com
www.mark-magazine.com

Editorial
Editor in Chief
Arthur Wortmann
arthur@frameweb.com

Editor
David Keuning
david@frameweb.com

Editorial Intern
Lauren Teague
laurenteague@frameweb.com

Contributing Editors
Thomas Daniell, Grant Gibson,
Florian Heilmeyer, Cathelijne
Nuijsink, Katya Tylevich,
Michael Webb

Contributing Photographer
Sergio Pirrone

Copy Editors
InOtherWords (D'Laine Camp,
Donna de Vries-Hermansader)

Design Director
Barbara Iwanicka

Designers
Cathelijn Kruunenberg
Zoe Bar-Pereg

Translators
InOtherWords (Donna de Vries-
Hermansader, Christine Gardner,
Jesse van der Hoeven, Rachel
Keeton, Maria van Tol)

Contributors to this issue
Izabela Anna, Michele Braidy,
Stefano Corbo, Theo Deutinger,
Rafael Gomez-Moriana, Kirsten
Hannema, Stephanie Hughes,
Ana Martins, Gili Merin,
Terri Peters, Oliver Zeller

Printing
Tuijtel

Lithography
Edward de Nijs

Cover Photography
Bahaa Ghoussainy

Publishing
Directors
Robert Thiemann
robert@frameweb.com
Rudolf van Wezel
rudolf@frameweb.com
David de Swaan
dds@frameweb.com

Distribution and Logistics
Manager
Nick van Oppenraaij
nick@frameweb.com

Sales Manager
Ed Smit
ed@frameweb.com

Finance
finance@frameweb.com

Advertising Representatives
Italy
Studio Mitos
Michele Tosato
michele@studiomitos.it
T +39 0422 894 868

Turkey
Titajans
Hilmi Zafer Erdem
titajans@titajans.com
T +90 212 257 76 66

Subscriptions
If you have a question about
your subscription, please email
subscriptions@frameweb.com
or call us at +31 85 888 3551

Subscription Rates
Including VAT and postage within
the EU and Switzerland.

6-months (3 issues): €49
1-year (6 issues): €99
1-year student* (6 issues): €79
2-year (12 issues): €188

To subscribe, visit
www.mark-magazine.com

* valid only with a copy of your student
registration form

Bookstore Distributors
Mark is available at sales points
worldwide.

Back Issues
Buy online at store.frameweb.com

Mark (ISSN: 1574-6453, USPS No:
019-372) is published bi-monthly
by Frame Publishers NL and
distributed in the USA by Asendia
USA, 17B S Middlesex Ave,
Monroe NJ 08831. Periodicals
postage paid New Brunswick, NJ
and additional mailing offices.
Postmaster: send address changes
to *Mark*, 701C Ashland Ave,
Folcroft PA 19032.

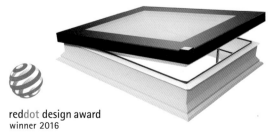

Notiice
Board

'There's a fundamental longing for

Christoph Hesse and Neeraj Bhatia at the 'Ways of Life' exhibition in Kassel, page 014

nature, evoked by the contemporary challenges of urbanity'

Rendering by *Art-Invest / Accumulata Immobilien*   2

1

1   **Retirement Housing**
Chonburi – Thailand
ASWA (Architectural Studio of
Work-Aholic)
– A 3,500-m² retirement home
with heath facilities
Expected completion undisclosed
aswarchitect.com

2   **Die Macherei**
Munich – Germany
Hollwich Kushner, OSA Ochs
Schmidhuber and MSM Meyer
Schmitz-Morkramer
– Urban centre with 64,000
m² of rental space, including a
hotel, offices and incubator space
for Art-Invest and Accumulata
Immobilien
Expected completion 2019
hwkn.com
osa-muenchen.de
msm-architecture.com

3   **Contemporary Hamlet**
Limoges – France
CoCo Architecture
– Forty housing units, car park
and workshop
*Competition entry, 1ˢᵗ prize,
expected completion 2019*
cocoarchitecture.fr

4   **Quartier Heidestrasse**
Berlin – Germany
EM2N
– A row of commercial buildings
with two office headquarters, one
at the south end of Heidestrasse
and one at Nordhafenplatz, in
Europacity
*Competition entry, 1ˢᵗ prize,
expected completion undisclosed*
em2n.ch

Rendering by *Saida Dalmau (sbda.cat)*

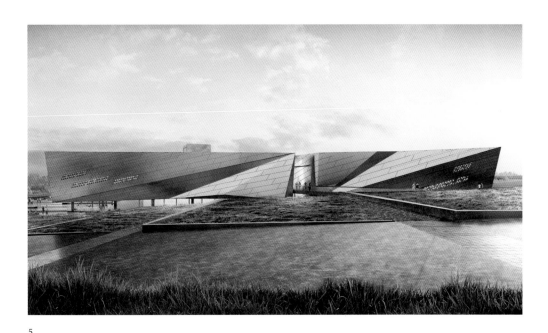

5

6

5 **Museum of Istanbul**
Istanbul – Turkey
Alper Derinboğaz
– A 38,000-m^2 museum
featuring the 8,000-year history
of Istanbul, with permanent
exhibition spaces, library,
children's workshop, event hall,
activity areas, restaurants, cafés
and temporary exhibition hall
Expected completion 2018
salonarchitects.com

6 **Antelias 1403**
Antelias – Lebanon
J.M.Bonfils Architects
– A 60,000-m^2 mixed-use project
with retail and offices
Expected completion undisclosed
jmbonfils.com

7 **Grand Egyptian Museum**
Giza – Egypt
Heneghan Peng Architects
(architecture) and Atelier
Brückner (exhibition design)
– A 90,000-m^2 museum,
currently under construction
near the Great Pyramids of Giza
*Competition entry, 1st prize,
expected completion undisclosed*
hparc.com
atelier-brueckner.com

7

Ways of Life

As part of Documenta 14, the 'Ways of Life' exhibition appeared in July at the Kulturbahnhof in Kassel, Germany. Twenty architects presented twenty designs for buildings that combine living and working within nature. The proposed sites are in Scheid, a peninsula that extends into the Edersee, a lake in central Germany. The curators, Christoph Hesse and Neeraj Bhatia, hope to find clients for some of the houses and have them built. After it closed at the end of July, the exhibition moved to the foyer of the University of Kassel's ASL Building, where it can be visited until 17 September.

1

2

3

4

5

Rendering by Squarevoxel

1   **House of Endless Landscapes**
Atelier Alter (Yingfan Zhang, Xiaojun Bu, Kai Qin, Zhenwei Li, Lidong Song, Jiahe Zhang and Ran Yan)
atelieraltercn.com

2   **Eder**
Pezo Von Ellrichshausen
pezo.cl

3   **Yin Yang House**
Penda
home-of-penda.com

4   **Earth Wind Water House**
Christoph Hesse Architects
christophhesse.eu

5   **Perched House**
Somatic Collaborative (Felipe Correa, James Carse, Anthony Acciavatti, Clayton Strange and Jessy Yang)
somatic-collaborative.com

6   **Workshop Recovering Humanism**
Yamazaki Kentaro Design
ykdw.org

7   **Ten Stories' House**
Rica Studio (Iñaqui Carnicero, Lorena del Río and Antonio Boeri)
ricastudio.com

8   **Depth of Fields**
The Open Workshop (Neeraj Bhatia, Hayfa Al-Gwaiz, Jared Clifton, Cesar Lopez, Nicholas Scribner and Laura Williams)
theopenworkshop.ca

6

7

8

Renderings by Arq&DEA

1

2

**1   CNAD (Centro Nacional
de Artesanato e Design)**
Mindelo – São Vincente –
Cape Verde
Ramos Castellano Arquitectos
(Moreno Castellano and
Eloisa Ramos)
– Design museum
Expected completion 2019
ramoscastellano.com

3

2   De Voortuinen
Amsterdam – Netherlands
Tank Architecture
– A 9,000-m² apartment tower
in a former office building
Expected completion 2018
tank.nl

3   Extension Fondation Beyeler
Basel – Switzerland
Atelier Peter Zumthor
– Extension to art museum
Fondation Beyeler, to be realized
in the Iselin-Weber Park
Expected completion undisclosed
fondationbeyeler.ch

IT'S ROBERTO, GIORDANO, LORETTA AND DAVIDE WHO MAKE ITALIAN CERAMICS SO SPECIAL

CERAMICS OF ITALY. ITALIANS MAKE THE DIFFERENCE.

It's Italians who make the difference. Like Roberto, Giordano, Loretta and Davide who work hard every day to ensure that Italian ceramics are the finest in the world. Only the very best manufacturers of Italian ceramic tiles, sanitaryware and tableware are entitled to use the Ceramics of Italy logo which certifies Italian quality, design and style. Always ask for Ceramics of Italy to be sure of the highest levels of excellence in world ceramics.

laceramicaitaliana.it

Ceramics of Italy

1

1 Danish National Rowing Stadium
Copenhagen – Denmark
AART Architects, E+E Architects and LIW Planning
– National rowing stadium at Bagsværd Lake, including a referee tower and a rowing centre with boat hall, workshop, training room, multipurpose room, meeting rooms and administration
Expected completion 2020
aart.dk

2

2 Hospital of the Future
Martin – Slovakia
FAAB (Adam Białobrzeski, Adam Figurski and Maria Messina)
– University hospital with an emergency and trauma centre, laboratory complex, diagnostic unit, transplantation centre, surgery centre, internal-medicine centre, women-mother-baby centre, rehabilitation centre and more
Competition entry, 3rd prize
faab.pl

Cross Section

'We talk about flow in architecture, but as architects, we do build boundaries'

Matteo Ghidoni of Salottobuono about his temporary pavilion in Mexico City, page 024

Full-bodied Red

Extrastudio converted a winery into a home.

Text Ana Martins
Photos Fernando Guerra / FG+SG

Lisbon-based Extrastudio combined age-old construction techniques and existing materials with the clean lines of contemporary architecture to turn a family-owned winery into a home. Located in Vendas de Azeitão, a small village 40 km south of the Portuguese capital, the 360-m² Red House was completed in 2016.

In its exploration of Mediterranean imagery and the accompanying lifestyle, landscape firm Oficina dos Jardins decided to preserve a grove of orange trees at the site and to add a reflective swimming pool. According to João Ferrão of Extrastudio, the 'microclimate' of the garden enters the ground-floor living area through a 14-m-long glazed section on the west side of the house, causing the interior and exterior to merge.

How did the design evolve?
JOÃO FERRÃO: On our first visit to the site, we were struck by the winery. The façade was covered in lichens, like the surface of a rock. That's when we started thinking of combining an ageing and altering exterior with a more fixed, contemporary interior. Because the volume of the building far exceeded the programme required for the house, we realized that what we had in mind couldn't occupy the existing two floors in their entirety. Instead, we created a hierarchy of double- and triple-height spaces.

Can you explain why you adopted this particular reuse strategy?
We saw much of the project's potential in the original construction, which we had to either maintain or transform. We might have missed the opportunity to work with quicklime if we hadn't had to deal with elements that were manufactured and used at a previous time and were, therefore, incompatible with today's techniques. Certainly, it would have been a crime not to make use of the roof tiles, timber and stone that were available on site.

Why did you choose red for the façade?
The shade we used is identical to the red of Alcázar of Seville's Lion Gate – even the technique and material are the same. In the early 20th century, as industrial paints became available, the older techniques were abandoned without ever questioning their utility. This house will never have to be painted, and its colour will be in permanent transformation.
extrastudio.pt

Cross Section

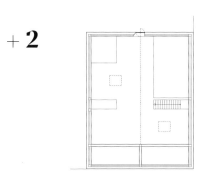

+ 2

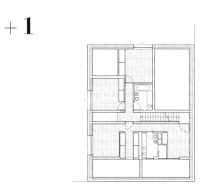

+ 1

0

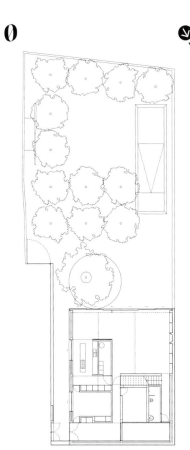

A triple-height void connects the living room to the attic.

Writing on the Wall

Matteo Ghidoni designed a room full of interpretations.

Architect Matteo Ghidoni says his temporary pavilion – the result of an international competition – contained a 'fragment of desert'.
Photo Juan Benavides

Photo LGM Studio / Luis Gallardo

Text Katya Tylevich

'When "the wall" is all people can think about, then okay, maybe it's time to think about the wall,' says Matteo Ghidoni, the founder of Salottobuono. The Milan architecture studio collaborated with Venice-based Enrico Dusi for the realization – and near-instant demolition, two weeks later – of a temporary pavilion called A Room, which appeared at Mextrópoli, an international architecture festival in Mexico City.

Three 4-m-high concrete walls, one equipped with a basketball hoop, bordered the 43-m² triangular Room, which people entered through a human-sized hole (2 m in diameter) or a ladder propped against the exterior. A hole 60 cm in diameter invited them to peep inside. A slope of desert sand ending in a copse of cacti represented what many of us envision when we think of what's 'across the border'.

Maybe the structure is architectural satire on you-know-who's big, beautiful – *very, very* beautiful – flavour of the day, but Ghidoni almost sighs when I mention his name. 'Yes, yes, but we thought it a bit cynical and easy to end there.' One

critic judged A Room to be a commentary on colonialism, and, oh my God, what isn't? But the pavilion can also be seen as an introspective contemplation of architecture's contemporary role.

'Room is almost an archetype,' says Ghidoni, 'You define a space with walls and establish a difference between outside and inside.' This pavilion's interior, however, is a slice of the outside (the wild, the past), while its urban outdoors are completely designed and man-made. 'We talk about flow in architecture – the movement of

bodies – but as architects, we do build boundaries,' he says, drawing attention to architecture as an artifice of freedom in confined zones. Then again, A Room pays homage to Luis Barragán and the modernists. Ultimately, the work is a wide reflection on the urban condition *and* an experiment. 'I almost hoped it would be vandalized,' he says with disappointment, 'but people treated it very well.'

salottobuono.com

Sports Complex Koning Willem-Alexander by Slangen+Koenis

concrete skin

| sustainable glassfibre reinforced concrete

| non-combustible and maintenance free

| natural and durable material, authentic appearance

| various colours and shapes, vivid surface

www.rieder.cc

RIEDER

Window of Opportunity

Ryu Mitarai uses bay windows to produce additional floor space.

Text Cathelijne Nuijsink
Photos Kai Nakamura

What is your interest in the window, a basic architectural element?
RYU MITARAI: I am particularly interested in the possibilities of scale provided by the window, which initially functioned as an opening for the passage of light and air. But if we enlarge the window and give it depth, it can be used as a space-making element. As such, the window is released from modernist functionalism.

Did the making of spaces around the windows in this house stem from your client's request?
The client is a classmate from university. He and his family love the surrounding neighbourhood.

They requested brightness inside the house and the maximum floor area permitted on this site. In Japan, bay windows do not necessarily count as floor area by law. The client's requests, together with the gap in the law, gave me a big opportunity, which I used to design spaces around the windows.

Each of the seven bay windows seems to imply a different activity. Can you explain?
The window on the first floor facing the street serves as a gallery, with a view to the outside. The family likes to bring their portable tatami mats here to generate the feeling of a comfortable, traditionally Japanese

+ 2

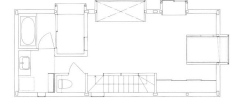

+ 1

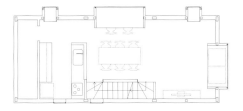

0

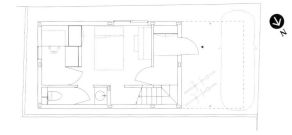

Long Section

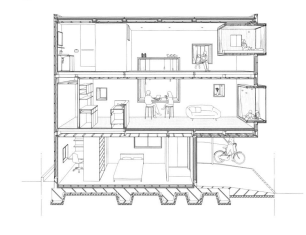

The biggest of the seven bay windows creates a void between the living room on the first floor and the children's room on the second floor.
Photo Yohei Imahori

space. Thanks to a light in the small window on the same floor, at night the entire bay window becomes a lighting fixture. The largest window, which connects the first and second floors, creates a void inside the house, where it is also used as a work counter. The small window next to the kitchen is sometimes used as a desk for the cook. A bay window on the second floor contains a bed that offers a view of the neighbourhood. A bench window finished with sound-absorbing wood wool cement board is a perfect spot for reading. Lastly, a window positioned outside on the balcony works as a buffer zone between the bath and the outdoors.

ryumitarai.jp

Rough yet Refined

Elding Oscarson's museum extension employs
Corten steel to create a distinctive contrast.

Interior walls are lined in birch plywood panels.

Plan

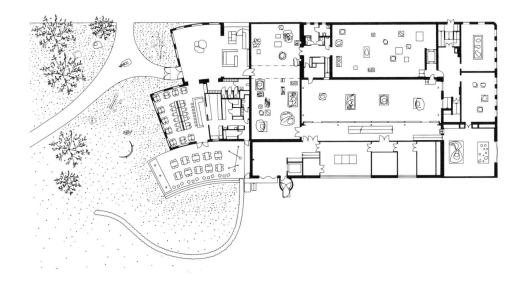

Section

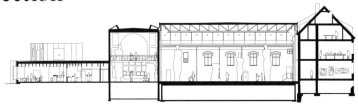

Text Lauren Teague
Photos Åke E:son Lindman

Founded in 1934 as the Museum of Artistic Process and Public Art, the Skissernas Museum in Lund, Sweden, features an archive that documents the artistic process and holds the world's largest collection of sketches, templates and models. In its 70-year history, the building has seen countless visitors and exhibitions, plus a handful of architectural renovations, the most recent of which was realized earlier this year by Stockholm-based Elding Oscarson, a firm led by Jonas Elding and Johan Oscarson. It is the first time that the museum has incorporated separate facilities – foyer, restaurant, shop and multifunctional hall – for purposes other than exhibiting art. With the new extension, the architects hope to increase public interest in the museum as an attractive meeting place.

'Skissernas used to be the kind of museum that many people knew about and had visited once, but not the kind where you would go repeatedly,' says Elding. 'It was rather dormant, so to

speak.' The addition's rough façade, clad in Corten-steel panelling that gives the overall surface a slightly convex curve, timelessly complements the previous extension's brutalist concrete appearance. The architects selected Corten steel because it enabled the creation of sharply detailed panelling, a result quite unlike anything achievable in concrete. Visitors entering the building find a smooth skin of birch plywood that makes for a soft warm contrast. 'The wooden interior matches the outside in its detailing,' says Elding. 'It speaks a similar language, as well as emphasizing the presence of the outdoors inside the building.'

External walls are interspersed with windows that suggest random placement. In fact, their carefully calculated positions offer specific views of the surrounding landscape and open sightlines throughout the building, providing a level of transparency without resorting to conventional curtain glazing.

eldingoscarson.com

A New Media Shell

In the film *Ghost in the Shell*, the cityscape is determined by augmented-reality holograms – or 'solograms'.

Text Oliver Zeller
Images Paramount Pictures

Ghost in the Shell (1995) – an iconic anime film directed by Mamoru Oshii and based on Masumune Shirow's manga – remains a highly influential science fiction movie. Like the Japanese original, an American live-action remake of the same name explores the nature of consciousness and humanity in an age of robotics, artificial intelligence and cyberization. What may sound like fiction is becoming increasingly topical as we edge towards transhumanism, exemplified by Elon Musk's recent launch of brain-augmentation venture Neuralink.

In this year's *Ghost in the Shell*, Section 9 counterterrorism commander Mira Killian becomes the first human to successfully undergo a brain implant into a cybernetic body, courtesy of Hanka Robotics. When Section 9 responds to a hacker who violently disrupts a Hanka meeting, the team gradually unveils a conspiracy.

In transitioning *Ghost in the Shell* to live action, director Rupert Sanders (*Snow White and the Huntsman*) and production designer Jan Roelfs (*Gattaca*) produce a visually striking film that derives much of its character from 1980s Hong Kong. The Paul Rudolph-designed Lippo Centre serves as Hanka headquarters, and a more angular redesign of the windowless Hong Kong Cultural Centre by government architect Pau Shiu-hung becomes Section 9's base of military operations. Monolithic concrete buildings designed by Ash Thorp, Maciej Kuciara and Weta Workshop loosely follow the same aesthetic. Their aim was to 'echo the look of a mainframe computer'. Stacked and cascading architecture is a common refrain, from the Montane Mansion and Tsuen Wan Chinese Permanent Cemetery to the bi-cyclindrical skyscrapers of public housing estate Lai Tak Tsuen.

In Thom Bettridge's interview with curator Stefan Riekeles, they discuss the architecture in the original anime, in which Hong Kong was used to depict the Japan of the future. According to Riekeles: 'The idea was to evoke a feeling of submerging into the deep levels of the city, where a flood of information overflows the human senses and a lot of noise surrounds the people.' The 2017 film rouses this feeling with 'solograms': 'virtual, augmented-reality holograms where objects on different scales exist, animate, and interact with an environment' and where everyone 'sees the city differently'. Signage dynamically extends into three dimensions, and otherwise mundane architecture is transformed by adverts that can be as tall as a building, producing a 'sensory overload' that conjures the 'carnivalesque feel' of the 2004 anime sequel, *Ghost in the Shell 2: Innocence.*

Solograms aren't a particularly new concept. Last year's Syfy series, *Incorporated*, showcased such visuals, as did Keiichi Matsuda's short film, *Hyper-Reality*. Yet solograms in the 2017 film seem to redefine architecture, eliciting questions of how architects, urban planners and artists can leverage media to define a building's shell, while still maintaining its ghost.

Enrico Montecchi - Fabrizio Mariani
NABA - Nuova Accademia di Belle Arti, Milano.

CERSAIE

25-29 SEPTEMBER 2017

BOLOGNA ■ ITALY

INTERNATIONAL EXHIBITION OF CERAMIC TILE AND BATHROOM FURNISHINGS

promoted by

 CONFINDUSTRIA CERAMICA

in collaboration with

Bologna Fiere

Free ticket online
www.cersaie.it/onlinebooth

organized by

EdiCer· SpA

show management
Promos srl

Galvanized Diamond

Christ & Gantenbein provides Pratteln with a landmark.

Text <u>Lauren Teague</u>
Photo <u>Stefano Graziani</u>

Aquila Tower, designed by Swiss outfit Christ & Gantenbein, is based on a traditional form: a tower atop a podium. The mixed-use complex is in the municipality of Pratteln, some 10 km southeast of central Basel. Nearly a quarter of the area's built environment comprises industrial buildings or urban infrastructure.

The architects manipulated the form of the high-rise in order to reduce the effects of noise pollution from the neighbouring railway without the need for a costly double façade. The lower levels of Aquila Tower, which accommodate retail and office space, are split into pointed wings that open towards the train station, seemingly drawing visitors into a welcoming two-armed embrace. Inside the 20-storey residential tower, 76 apartments fan out from a northern access core, maximizing exposure to the southern perimeter and diminishing the risk of noise disturbance as the tower turns its back on the railway. A diamond-shaped floor plan and 'squinting' windows that offer wide views of the surroundings are part of Christ & Gantenbein's strategy for affording comfort to occupants.

The project's galvanized-steel skin, which refers directly to the industrial character of the area, is intended to weather gracefully. 'Untreated steel plates would eventually rust, but galvanization ensures effective protection,' say the architects. 'That said, the surface remains reactive and is subject to changes in colour as a result of environmental conditions. The material's appearance can change unexpectedly within a matter of weeks or even days.'

christgantenbein.com

Cross Section

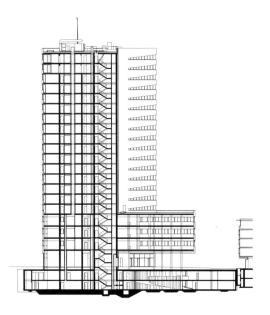

+ **18**

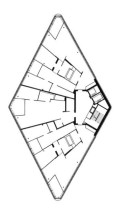

+ **4**

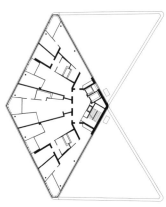

+ **1**

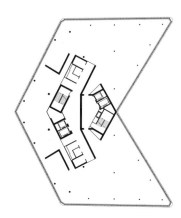

0

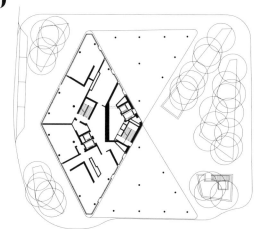

Child's Play

Rosenbaum and Aleph Zero provide students with light, air and space.

Text Ana Martins
Photos Leonardo Finotti

In a rural area of Brazil's Central-West Region, the Bradesco Foundation set up its first boarding school in 1973. Since then, Fazenda de Canuaña has hosted children from remote villages that offer no opportunities for a formal education. The school's new residences, completed in 2016, are part of a 30-year master plan being carried out by São Paulo-based studio Rosenbaum to revamp the entire complex.

For this project, studio founder Marcelo Rosenbaum approached Gustavo Utrabo and Pedro Duschenes of Aleph Zero, another Paulista architecture firm. Together they embarked on a design process guided by three principles featured in Rosenbaum's manifesto, 'A Gente Transforma': ancestry, beauty and sustainability.

The statement refers to architecture and design created to reconnect with age-old traditions in remote areas of Brazil.

During two stays in Canuaña, the architects visited the children's native villages, spoke to parents and educators, engaged with members of the indigenous Javaé tribe and, through workshops with the pupils, tried to understand what would make the boarding school feel more like home.

By analysing the children's relationship with space and initiating a dialogue to discover their ideas for the new residences, the architects arrived at the dimensions and shapes of the various rooms and determined what sort of complementary spaces would be necessary. Each 11,500-m² building (one for boys,

To avoid having the school stand out like an unsightly blot on the landscape, the architects blurred the boundaries between inside and outside.

one for girls) contains 45 rooms, each with six beds, and communal facilities such as TV and reading rooms, balconies and courtyards.

Utrabo's goal was to 'translate the region's complex culture and history into architecture'. Although the traditional adobe and straw homes of farmers living in camps are extremely effective in terms of isolation and ventilation – the region has a tropical climate – they are seen as substandard constructions. To raise awareness of their value, Rosenbaum and Aleph Zero used some 4,000 adobe bricks, made on site, for the walls of the new buildings. Small openings supply natural ventilation and give the façades a dynamic aesthetic. Finally, after several conversations with tribal leaders, they developed a written and graphic vocabulary for use in indicating the rooms, each of which has a Javaé name and corresponding graphic panel.

The resulting residences provide pupils with warm and welcoming spaces that help them find their individuality within a collective environment. The school is also a generous source of ancestral and indigenous culture, values and traditions. In Rosenbaum's words: 'We were looking to reconnect the children with the wealth of the area's history.' He believes that architecture can 'heal' old perceptions and restore the use of timeworn skills. It should never be 'an imposition'.

alephzero.arq.br
rosenbaum.com.br

+1

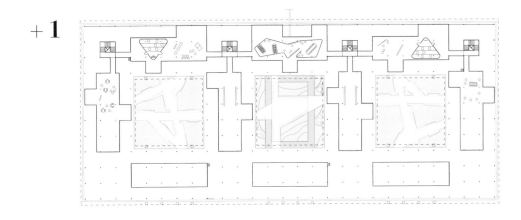

0

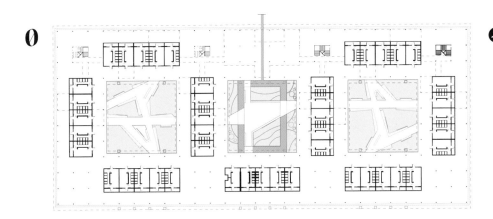

Sections

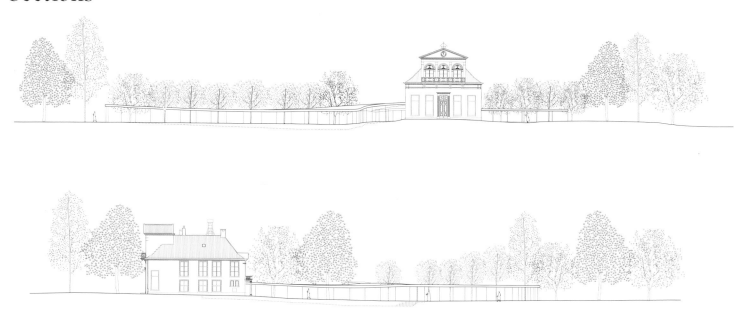

The pavilion emerges from a single
plate of glass.

Long Section

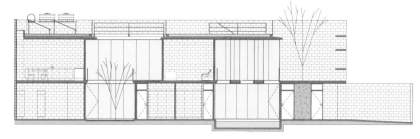

+ 1

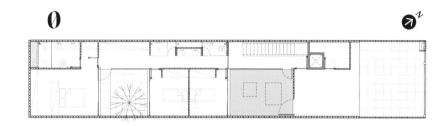

0

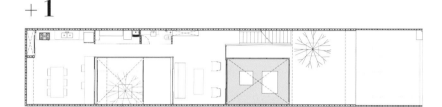

a balanced path between the ideas of our client and the city environment. The building is 6 m tall and with the rooftop's terrace safety wall it reaches 7 m. That was the maximum height allowed at the time of the design.

At the end of 2016, a law was passed that increased the allowed building height to 10 m. Real estate development is now in full swing and we estimate that in less than ten years, the area will be completely different. São Paulo is a city that does not keep or preserve, at the very best it longs for what once was. Decade after decade a new city emerges, in a movement that is invisible to the eyes of society.

How did the collaboration with landscape architect Gabriella Ornaghi develop?

PEDRO TUMA: We began to work together early on, allowing us to arrive at solutions that would otherwise have been impossible. Two fundamental examples are the foliage trays over the fish pond, and the tree planted on the first-floor balcony. In the first instance, slabs had to be calculated to carry their load and in the second, a vertical tunnel filled with soil was developed so that the roots could develop naturally.

In your opinion, what is the project's main characteristic?

FERNANDA SAKANO: Even though they are not new to the world of architecture, proposing solutions such as the inversion of the interior/exterior dichotomy, or placing the private spaces on the ground floor – whereas traditionally that would be the location of the social areas – was not an easy task. Our intention is to always keep an open dialogue with society in order to move forward, instead of maintaining a comfortable position of conformity. We believe that small things like these, thanks to the direct relationship with our clients, are more edifying to the architectural profession than one might realize.

terraetuma.com

Foliage trays hover over the fish pond.

Acoustic Domesticity

Chance de Silva Architects and Scanner team up to design a residential sound.

Text Campbell McNeill
Photos Hélène Binet

Stephen Chance and Wendy de Silva started collaborating with sound artist Robin Rimbaud (aka Scanner) in 2012, setting out to explore the boundary between sound and architecture. To date they have exhibited work at the 2014 Venice Biennale; made recordings of the sound of pouring concrete; and designed Vex, a studio house in Stoke Newington, an area in the London borough of Hackney.

Buildings are usually designed with the human senses in mind – sight being the most important – but some typologies lend themselves to a focused consideration of those senses: restaurants curate taste, baths provide textures and temperatures, gardens offer fragrance, galleries accommodate visual arts and concert halls are all about sound. Architects might have all five senses in mind when designing a house, but most often they focus on visual articulation and spatial organization. In the case of Vex, Chance de Silva and Scanner overlaid functions in an assemblage that can be experienced not only as a continuous volume and a visual spectacle, but also as an environment for listening.

The house is on a street in a Victorian conservation area and came with a challenging set of contextual requirements. Instead of taking cues from the surroundings, the team drew inspiration from Erik Satie's *Vexations*, an 18-hour-long (sometimes even longer) piano piece written in the late 19th century that features a short theme replayed 840 times. The architects and sound artist introduced Satie's repetition conceptually by wrapping a design model in the musical score, leaving

The three-storey building houses a ground-floor studio and living spaces on the upper levels.

Roof

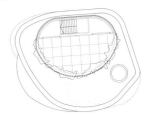

+2

+1

0

marks translated into vertical ridges. Exterior walls are concrete cast *in situ* using corrugated formwork that gives the building its soft, fluted, rhythmic materiality. The re-looping of the musical work is referenced with elliptical floors stacked and shifted to create a winding circulation plan, as well as a number of vertical openings that allow light to enter the interior, where space and acoustics can blend into a stage for performances, as Stephen Chance explains. 'At some point we are going to have a live gig here,' he says, 'where Scanner will mix construction sounds recorded during the project.'

chancedesilva.com

Long Section

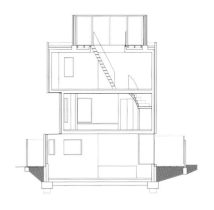

Moose Tower is the first of five projects planned for the area.
The second, a walkway in the gorge, is currently under construction.
The remaining three have yet to find financial backing.

Into the Wild

Six beds cantilever into the treetops from Ram Arkitektur's log tower in Norway.

+ 3

+ 2

+ 1

Text <u>Lauren Teague</u>
Photos <u>Sam Hughes</u>

Long Section

The accommodation includes a small communal area on the third level, with a wood stove and cooking facilities.

Plans for the Norwegian valley of Espedalen include a series of five architectural interventions intended to entice motorists to stop and explore the area. With funding provided by two local hotels (Ruten Fjellstue and Dalseter Høyfjellshotell), the first project to be completed is Elgtårn (Moose Tower), a 12-m-high lakeside structure topped by a viewing platform. Providing only the bare bones of hospitality, Elgtårn offers overnight accommodation for six visitors – but no running water or electricity. Beds cantilevering from three sides of the tower are protected from the treetops by panes of glass. On the remaining side, ladders to the viewing platform add a sense of drama to the climb.

What is the project about?
SAM HUGHES (Ram Arkitektur): The idea was to create a unique overnight experience for a small number of guests in a remote location, combined with a public viewing platform. The form of the building emerged through early sketches aimed at the efficient placement of beds around a small space. We wanted each bed to have a panoramic view of the surrounding area.

How did the construction phase go?
The remote location made access to the site difficult. By using modular elements, we reduced the amount of production work required on site, as well as the number of materials being transported. We explored different types of prefabricated

panels throughout the design phase. During one of our early site visits with the client, we looked at some of the historical buildings in the valley and the idea crystallized – a real eureka moment – that a log-type construction made sense. Its long history and strong connection with the valley satisfied all the criteria for the modular system we were trying to develop. The overall aesthetic is a result of the structural principles we applied. The influence of local traditions firmly anchors the identity of the tower into its regional context, even though we interpreted the past in the form of a contemporary design.

ram-arkitektur.no

Expansive Living

Suppose Design Office creates
openness by building walls.

0   **↻z**   **+1**   **+2**

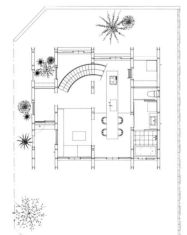

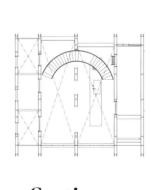

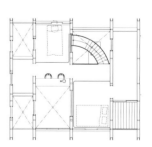

Cross Section

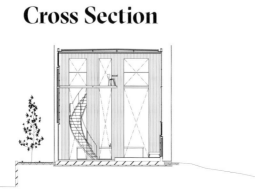

Long Section

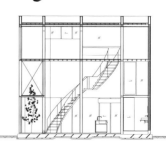

The interior of the house is a continuous space that is subtly divided into smaller spaces.

Text Cathelijne Nuijsink
Photos Toshiyuki Yano

<u>Did your clients have a clear vision of what their new house should be?</u>
MAKOTO TANIJIRI (Suppose Design Office): The couple and their two children used to live in a typical Japanese condominium with an interior that was difficult to open fully. It's that limitation that led to their request for a house with 'a feeling of openness'.

<u>Why do you believe that walls are the best way to create openness?</u>
Without 'closeness', 'openness' does not have meaning. In this house, we used five walls arranged in parallel to achieve a simultaneous condition of open and closed. Openness is generated through the making of apertures, or 'walls with openings', which form layers that introduce a sense of depth into the space. As a result, you feel more openness in this house than you would if there were no walls. Call it a 'sensation of unending expansiveness'. Although not obviously divided into rooms, the interior has a sense of continuity and separation at the same time.

<u>Although the concept fits into your portfolio as a project that combines what you call 'inconsistent elements' – in this case openness and closeness – what makes it stand out from your other residential projects?</u>
We deliberately used a minimum number of architectural elements to make a maximum impact. I believe that by limiting the amount of elements and by considering the scale of the building – in terms of small and large, narrow and wide, high and low – we can better define a new kind of space.

suppose.jp

Model House

Studio MK27's latest house is exemplary in more than one way.

Text Ana Martins
Photos Fernando Guerra / FG+SG

A self-sufficient, modular dwelling that does not impose on the surrounding nature. This was the client's request when he approached Márcio Kogan, founder of São Paulo-based Studio MK27, to design a model house for one of the plots on his Catuçaba estate.

During a process that lasted five years, architects Márcio Kogan and Lair Reis developed their design, which they characterize as 'modernist Caipira' (a sort of modern local farm). They adapted it to the wishes of new owners and oversaw the construction of the first Catuçaba

House: a 309-m² pre-fabricated FSC wood structure nestled between two adobe brick walls.

Sloping and remote, the site was but one of the challenges that the architects faced. As they worked towards a self-sufficient design, the dwelling was chosen as a pilot project for the development of sustainability reference standards for houses in Brazil. Building according to LEED standards meant that the architects had to not only take the house's energy performance into consideration, but also the sustainability of the materials and construction methods used.

The bedrooms' small openings are a reinterpretation of the blue colonial windows found throughout the area.

A north-facing balcony that stretches along the house's entire width looks out onto the vast expanse of the estate.

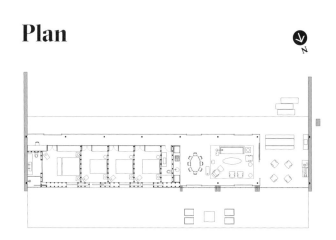

The living room has glass walls on three sides.

The open kitchen, dining and living area is surrounded by double-glazed openings and protected by folding eucalyptus wood shutters on the south-facing front. When closed, the latter forms a continuation of the wooden façade of the sleeping area, which contains four bedrooms. The interior floors are lined in adobe brick, and the grass-covered roof is fitted with solar thermal and photovoltaic panels. PET foam insulation, natural ventilation and a wind turbine further contribute to the house's efficiency and self-sufficiency.

The architects saw in the project – the first house to receive the highest level of Brazil's Green Building Council (GBC) certification – an opportunity to further the studio's knowledge and culture of sustainable development. 'From now on, every home we design will reach the minimum level of GBC certification at no additional costs to the client,' Reis maintains. 'Depending on the client's interests and budget, we can then work to achieve a higher certification.'
studiomk27.com

Plan

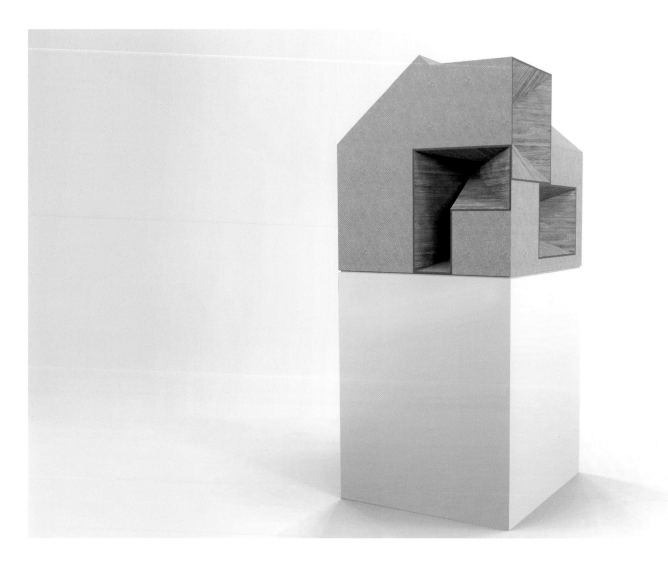

M3H

Text Kirsten Hannema

Dutch architect Peter Masselink always wanted to build a dollhouse for his youngest daughter Juliet. He didn't get to make one for his first, Imre: she died shortly after birth of a mitochondrial disease, the same rare disease that afflicts his son Sverre (7 years old), for which there is still no cure. It was this tragic circumstance that brought back the idea of the dollhouse, and he invited 17 colleagues to join him in designing a contemporary version of this time-honoured toy. They will be auctioned off this fall, with the proceeds going to two charities that support the research of mitochondrial diseases. A similar British dollhouse project in 2013, which featured famous architects like Zaha Hadid, generated over 100,000 euros.

The dollhouse project is more than a benefit, it is also an exploration of the dollhouse as an object for playing, learning,

exploration and art, inspired by the sick child's realm. The results vary greatly. M3H came up with the Listening House, an archetypical house with rooms as speakers that play compositions with 'homey' sounds. Dreessen Willemse Architects thought up a construction box that children can use to build their own dream house (or boat, or train). Office Winhov designed a cross between Petronella Oortman's 17th-century dollhouse in the Amsterdam Rijksmuseum and the pavilion Friedrich Schinkel built for Friedrich Wilhelm III in 1825 in the gardens of Charlottenburg Palace. Masselink himself made a suspended, egg-shaped dollhouse for his kids. Sverre, who has multiple disabilities, can play with the Escher-like interior that is hidden in the half open construction while lying down.

dolls-house.nl

Office Winhov

Inside Life

Seventeen dollhouses to invigorate a child's world.

Sverre Group

Dreessen Willemse Architects

Perspective

'<u>The dynamics of appropriating public domain in Beirut are individual</u>, <u>temporary</u>, agile and <u>weirdly inviting</u>'

Stephanie Akkaoui Hughes about the Lebanese capital, page 054

Look

But

Do citizens have an intrinsic right to their city? In Beirut, this question is not as rhetorical as it may seem.

Text
Stephanie Akkaoui Hughes

Having grown up in Beirut, for years I witnessed a constant dance of appropriation and negotiation of public space. Aided by moderate weather, public space in Lebanon's capital appears to be up for grabs. Anyone can, at any time, pull up a chair to smoke shisha on the pavement, play a game of *dama* with a friend on a street corner, or set up a number of tables to create a spontaneous extension to a local café. When walking on the streets – few of which even have pavements – you have to watch out for cars, street 'settlers' and private homes encroaching on the public domain. Daily and naturally, the city's inhabitants navigate such hazards. They apparently negotiate public space instinctively, along with others who are doing the same thing. The dynamics of appropriating public domain are individual, temporary (even if daily), agile and weirdly inviting. It's tempting to pull up a chair and join the party. To an outsider, these mechanisms may seem chaotic, even hopeless, but they're at the core of urban life in Beirut.

The gravity of the situation takes a new turn when this 'up for grabs' principle becomes accessible to commercial developers, whose basis for 'grabbing' is financial. Instead of a chair, their objective is a shopping mall, an office building or a residential high-rise, structures that are simply parachuted

onto a site which is in most cases – even if undeveloped – not empty or unused. The commercial settlements are larger, permanent and excluding. Throughout the history of urban development, city centres and downtown areas are usually a city's most heavily used public spaces. In Beirut, our Down Town – with a capital D and a capital T – is protected or controlled (a fine line divides the two) by armed guards. That should tell you enough.

Even though it may feel as if public space is everywhere, the reality is a total lack of public space in Beirut. Or, better said, there is no vision for and no protection of public space here. Almost daily, citizens are robbed of another plot of land, another view, another air space. No party is protecting the interests of citizens when it comes to the urban quality of the city. Public money is not public. There is no urban master plan and no overarching strategy for guiding developments towards making a unified city. Instead, we see the sporadic erection of individual projects driven by private interests, and as beautiful as they may or may not be, they are of little use to the city and its citizens. Beirut's urban development, in which private places and exclusive venues pop up regularly, can hardly be called gentrification. Or is it gentrification at all? Does gentrifying for another country's middle classes count?

Stacked terraced apartments, artists' studios, living lofts. Iconic structures, prime locations, priceless views. Who are these properties for? Can members of the emerging creative scene in Beirut – for which some projects are presumably designed – actually afford them? In fact, very few locals can pay to live in a residential tower. Most high-rise apartments are bought by Arabs from oil-rich countries in the Gulf who spend only a few weeks of the year in Beirut. An apartment in the sky allows them to escape the scorching heat and – equally often and not mutually exclusive – the social and cultural restrictions of neighbouring Gulf states. It's not gentrification that's happening here. Gentrifying a city for well-to-do visitors from another city doesn't count. What is happening is not even urban regeneration but rather the generation of a different city, a seasonal city, a city within a city.

Most of Beirut's high-rise sculptures are the work of local and foreign starchitects. Although they claim that the concepts behind these buildings emerged from the city itself, I believe their ideas are more often imposed on the city and its citizens. The way I see it, the incredibly rich history of Beirut is for foreign architects extremely 'exotic' and for our local ones an easy way out. Layers of occupation, years of civil war, gruesome assassinations in

Don't Touch

broad daylight and more recent wars all offer a mine rich in one-word concepts and one-liner responses. As a result, high-rises are frequently an exercise in stacking 'layers of history', reconnecting the worlds of inside and outside, commemorating bullet holes, shipwrecks and hand grenades. While it may be compelling and even intellectually witty at times, is it what the people of Beirut want to see as they negotiate public space? The concepts described here are not new, not exotic, not compelling and, I would argue, not helpful in an attempt to move forward. The developments themselves, as well as their concepts and aesthetics, are being imposed on citizens. What if such projects were to emerge through a participatory process that engages the population of Beirut? What if architecture was not a process of matter, but a matter of process?

We are operating in an era of starchitects. When a building is featured in magazines, it is celebrated, regardless of its consequences on the city and its citizens. Even when buildings do not physically displace families, they isolate and exclude by raising physical as well as social barriers. Describing

a tower as a 'vertical boulevard' does not make it one. A boulevard is a hub of social interactions; these towers are nothing more than an accumulation of shielded private worlds. Vegetation, gardens and green walls are recurrent themes in many new buildings in the city. I strongly doubt, however, that cladding a façade with a green wall is enough to claim that the community's been offered a garden that replaces an adjacent public garden once accessible to all. Although beautiful, the wall conveys a somewhat hypocritical 'look but don't touch' message.

In his four-volume masterwork, *The Nature of Order*, Christopher Alexander talks about the extent to which a building should support its surroundings. When he was involved in writing the zoning laws for an area in the USA, he included the requirement that an architect should demonstrate how a proposed building helps, supports or improves the surrounding environment. This item was strongly rejected by the zoning-laws board.

A recent study showed that all the architects in the world work for no more than 1 per cent of the global population. Most

architects are not aware of this fact and might even dispute its truth. Understandably, they find the information very disconcerting. It means that for 99 per cent of the world we architects are irrelevant, and we continue to narrow our target group. It's not that we're influencing fewer people. On the contrary, even though we cater for more exclusive groups, we influence – most of the time negatively and without considering the consequences – more and more people. In reaction to the adverse effect of our output, some of us wonder how we and our profession can remain relevant. It may be a perfectly acceptable question, but I think it's emanating from the wrong (egocentric) starting point. Why not look at the problem from an external perspective and ask how architecture can create added value? Can we evaluate good architecture by analysing not what it *is* but what it *does*? How does it serve the people inhabiting it, and how does it support those *not* inhabiting it? How does it help the larger community? How does it improve the quality of the city? ▂

Plan of Beirut

01 Bernard Khoury, Plot 1282, 2017
02 Bernard Khoury, Plot 4371, 2015
03 Herzog & de Meuron, Beirut Terraces, 2016
04 Youssef Tohme Architects, Villa M, 2017
05 Youssef Tohme Architects, Villa VR, 2017

05 Ajaltoun

04 Cornet Chahwan

03

Beirut

02 01

Jdeideh

Photo _Bahaa Ghoussainy_

In his architecture, Bernard Khoury no longer responds to future urban plans – they're bound to change anyway.

Text
Michele Braidy

'Beirut required from me that I answer in the now'

1993:

the war just ended in Lebanon, leaving the country an open wound. Beirut Central District is disfigured. The architectural future of the city is unclear. Despite the massive destruction, a strong hope rises among the new generation; the situation is seen as an opportunity for reconstruction and renewal. It is in this context that Bernard Khoury decides to come back to Beirut from the United States, where he's just graduated from Harvard University, and to start an independent architecture practice. His first projects mark this chaotic period through their straightforward and honest designs, while also generating controversy owing to their functions: he builds entertainment venues, for instance, at places with a rather macabre history, most notably the famous subterranean nightclub B018.

Almost 25 years later, Khoury runs a successful office that's involved in many of the city's noteworthy residential projects. Two recent examples are Plot #1282 and Plot #4371; Khoury often gives his Lebanese projects names that coincide with the Land Registry's plot numbers. Plot #1282 comprises 95 industrial lofts, most of which have double-height, open-plan living areas. Outside, the building's sharply edged terraces and expressive vertical lift shafts have a mysterious aesthetic and evoke images of a ghost ship. Plot #4371 is a compact, bullet-shaped, seven-storey building whose 29 units are also mainly double-height. The building's *pièce de résistance* is a large freight elevator that transports cars and motorcycles and allows them to be parked inside the apartments.

Bernard Khoury discusses the bumpy road that led from his early beginnings to his present-day ideas.

Your first projects were built on sites that were heavily charged with political history. The fact that they were meant to be temporary gave those projects even more intensity. Your discourse on scars and remembrance

Bernard Khoury.
Photo Piero Martinello

challenged the general denial of war and violence. Some of the early projects – now almost landmarks – remain today, but the context is quite different. When you consider your initial aims, do you recognize a sort of self-betrayal in the continuation of these projects?

BERNARD KHOURY: First, I would not use the word 'discourse'. I never had a systematic architectural strategy. I approach every project in a different way. You have to understand the political context that existed during that period. We had big hopes – call it naive – for the reconstruction of our nation. But it didn't happen, for many reasons. Our country has been hijacked by a corrupt, incompetent political class. Beirut Central District was completely privatized. For many of us architects, it was a very tough start. Architecture with a political dimension – social housing, schools or community centres, for instance – happens through institutional projects. At least that's what I had been taught during my academic years. But in Lebanon we couldn't build social projects. In this context, no political act was possible. In an attempt to survive, I had to explore other territories.

My clients handed me sites that hadn't reached full maturity in terms of land value; they wanted buildings for only a limited length of time. Because I couldn't design 'temporary' institutional projects, I started from the bottom up. I did a lot of entertainment venues, such as music clubs and bars, which are less meaningful on an architectural scale. There was a huge contradiction between the entertainment industry and the historically charged sites occupied by those venues. I had to deal with existential questions. To top it all off, my projects had predetermined expiry dates. To be honest, I had been obsessed with the notion of temporality even as a student, but being confronted with the ephemeral in post-war Beirut was a brutal experience for me. It's like telling a pregnant woman that her baby will die

'Beirut Central District has been hijacked by a corrupt, incompetent political class'

at the age of six. Nevertheless, I soon realized I could do something in temporary projects that I couldn't express otherwise. It changed my relation to time. Beirut required from me that I answer in the now and only the now, and I owe her that.

It's true that the present context is often completely different to what we initially found here. Restaurant-bar La Centrale has a roof that can be opened up. When we completed the project in 2001, the roof offered pretty views of old residential buildings in the vicinity. It's now surrounded by blank walls on three sides. The subterranean Yabani restaurant has simply been abandoned; the building is still there, but it's empty now. Beirut's reality has changed palpably. The gentrification of certain neighbourhoods endangers the coherence of such projects. Back in 2002, when Yabani was built, the building next to it was squatted by Syrian workers. Even the music we used to play at B018 was completely different. If B018 is still holding, it's because La Quarantaine is kind of cursed. The government stores mounds of garbage in that neighbourhood; no-one wants to settle in an environment like that. Although B018 has survived so far, it's still threatened by an expiry date. It's just a matter of time.

What is your approach to permanent projects?
My first permanent project, an apartment building called IB3 that was built in 2006, marked the beginning of a new phase for me. I've moved on from projects that didn't involve floor area ratios, for instance, to works that demand my compliance with that kind of stuff. To satisfy the requirements, I applied the city's zoning regulations to the letter. The form of the building corresponds to the maximum volume allowed. I didn't draw floor plans. I submitted the building for approval with a core and shell design, which included structure and circulation. I left the design of the floor plans and the façades to the interior architects. In my temporary projects, I had controlled everything

– right down to the tiniest furniture detail – and here I decided to let go of everything. The developers were more than happy. We now gear every project to its site, but we are also strongly inspired by the people who initiate these projects.

Indeed, in your book, _Local Heroes_, you focus on the close relationship between the story of a project, its site and its initiators. When you look at Plot #1282 and Plot #4371 from this perspective, what do you see?
Every site has its stumbling block. Plot #1282, in its present state, benefits from panoramic views, thanks to expansive glass façades and large balconies. Even though the area isn't residential at the moment, our project faces the risk of construction on surrounding plots that could literally suffocate it. Studying the history of plots in Beirut is like analysing the city's DNA. You begin to understand why we reached such a concentration of solitary islands with no possibility of communication between them. An unhealthy urban fabric leads to unhealthy living and feeds hostility among people. We applied a setback along the total perimeter and had the floor slabs gradually diminish as the building rises, allowing it to breathe and connect to its environment, even if it gets surrounded by other buildings.

As for Plot #4371, the developer had acquired this abandoned land – a property in line to be condemned – for a very good price. There wasn't a lot of interest initially, and I first refused to design a project that seemed destined to fail. But I couldn't resist the temptation of the developer's eccentric proposal for a high-rise designed for specific kinds of users: the divorced, the playboys, people without kids and those who liked the idea of ending the night in their cars, at home. It proved to be a winning bet. _

bernardkhoury.com

Plot #*1282*
Beirut — Lebanon — 2017

Containing 95 industrial lofts from 100 to 650 m², Plot #1282
occupies a total built-up area of 25,800 m². Nine exposed
cores lend access to a maximum of two apartments per floor.
Most units have double-height, open-plan living areas.

Photos Bahaa Ghoussainy

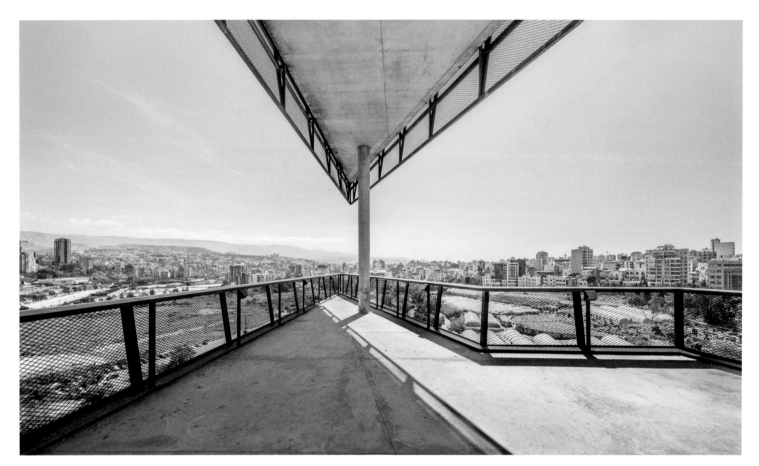

Generous balconies offer impressive views of the city – for now.

The ground floor houses an open-air car park.

The building site has a 430-m perimeter, only 12 m of which faces a public access road. The implication is that 97% of the perimeter borders on plots suitable for other building projects in the future.

Large balconies line the full perimeter of the building.

+ 5 upper level

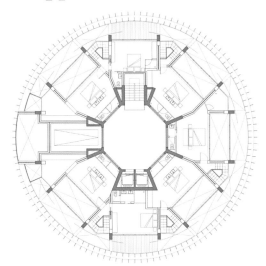

+ 5 lower level

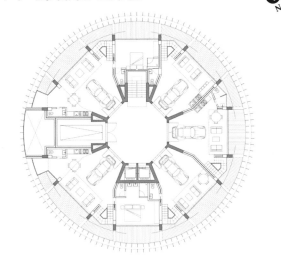

Section

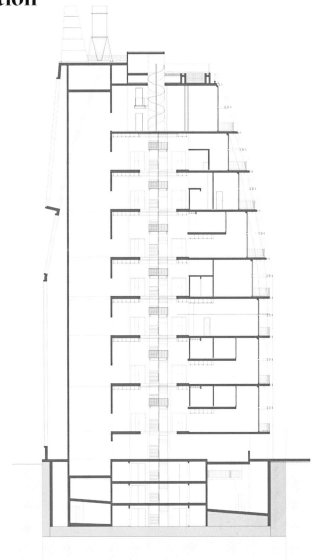

A freight elevator can be used to transport vehicles and other large loads.

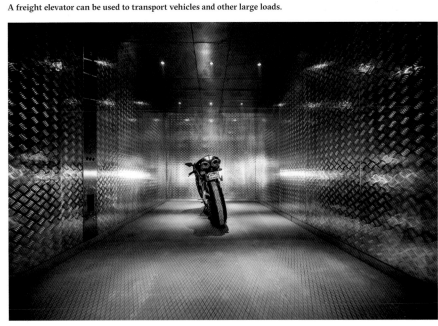

'An unhealthy urban fabric feeds hostility among people'

Stacking Layers

Although Herzog & de Meuron's Beirut Terraces project suggests transparency and permeability, it is first of all an accumulation of single luxury apartments.

Text
Stefano Corbo

Photos
Iwan Baan

Spacious terraces with glass balustrades are set back
from the edges of the floor slabs.

Opposite The entrance level is one storey above the street.

the beginning of the 1990s, with the Lebanese
Civil War finally over, Beirut's city centre
appeared to be a blank space, an involuntary
and promising tabula rasa upon which a new
model of coexistence could be based; around
80 per cent of the buildings had been destroyed
or seriously damaged. Through a series of
anomalous political concessions and procedural
faults, Solidere – a private company founded
by Rafik Hariri, Lebanon's prime minister at
the time – came to manage the entire process
of reconstruction of the Central District
and gradually became the only owner of the
area. An almost unique example of neoliberal
planning policies aimed at dismantling all
forms of public control over the urban fabric,
Solidere agreed to build Beirut's infrastructure,
including its collective utilities, in exchange for
a 75-year concession covering the management
of services and buildings, as well as the
construction of a new waterfront. International
firms invited to contribute to the master plan
realized residential and office towers for the
most part. To date, the regeneration of Beirut's
city centre is still not complete. Solidere has an
annual turnover equivalent to almost a quarter
of the Lebanese gross domestic product.

Beirut Terraces, Herzog & de Meuron's
first residential project in Lebanon, is part
of this complex and challenging context.
The 119-m-high tower is composed of 130
apartments on 26 levels. It was designed in
2009 with the cooperation of other established
firms: engineering consultant Arup, executive
architects Khatib & Alami, interior designer
Vincent Van Duysen and landscape architect
Vladimir Djurovic. In comparison with similar
projects built over the last few years in the
same area, Beirut Terraces is an attempt
to rethink the traditional typology of the
residential tower by offering an alternative
to the monotonous repetition of stacking
apartment units. At the same time, Herzog
& de Meuron's tower belongs to another
category of projects by the Swiss office, most
of them developed between 2005 and 2010
and characterized by a design methodology
that features an irregular and seemingly
unstable superposition of basic elements: boxes
(examples are 56 Leonard Street, 2016, and the
Actelion Business Center, 2005-2009), houses
(VitraHaus, 2006-2009), slabs (São Paulo
Cultural Complex Luz, 2009) and columns
(Bordeaux Stadium, 2011-2015). Manipulations,
variations and interaction among the
constitutive elements of these projects allowed

Herzog & de Meuron to experiment with
different languages of form and to reach an
unexpected outcome every time.

In Beirut, the asymmetric stratification
of 26 perforated white slabs produces a
diaphanous skeleton, an emptied tower
designed to be progressively integrated by
vegetation. The fluid space between slabs
generates a linear connection that joins
indoor and outdoor areas; the slabs of each
level protrude on all sides by a minimum of
60 cm to define terraces ranging from 28 m^2
to 400 m^2. Each slab acts as a homogenous
surface that merges interior and exterior.
Such an abstract and elegant overlaying of
slabs – the visual impact is reminiscent of
Mediterranean modernism from the 1950s – is
counterbalanced by a compact floor plan. The
organization of the building is the result of a
combination of five modular floors arranged
around a vertical core. The tower contains 60
two-bedroom units, 45 three-bedroom units,
17 four-bedroom units and eight duplexes
whose floor areas are between 615 m^2 and
985 m^2. Despite differences in size, all
apartments have a clear height of 3.31 m and
a sequence of three distinguishable areas: a
reception area with foyer and living room,
a private area with family spaces and
bedrooms, and a service area with kitchen
and laundry room. The programme also
includes communal amenities – spa, pool
and gym – as well as retail facilities and a
six-level underground car park. The vertical
core of the building accommodates lifts,
stairs and mechanical services. A structural
grid of columns that spans up to 14.7 m

precludes the need for loadbearing walls
inside the apartments and, in so doing, allows
for reconfiguration. The thick slabs not only
meet aesthetic considerations but also further
Herzog & de Meuron's passive design strategy
by maintaining the desired temperature
throughout the day, thus providing sustainable
thermal comfort.

Vegetal terrace walls separate the
apartments from one another and guarantee
an adequate level of privacy. Contrary to the
architects' desire for continuity and permeability,
isolation seems to be the key to this project:
isolation from the city as well as isolation
from one's neighbours. The spatial and formal
fragmentation of the tower is congruent with the
social condition of each occupant. Rather than a
'vertical village' (as the project was defined by its
developers), Beirut Terraces is an accumulation
of single luxury apartments: the sum of its
isolated units. If the use of vegetation is merely
defensive – a way to prevent social interaction
and preserve privacy – it's at street level where
the real character of the project reveals itself.
A sort of podium, decorated with plants and
surrounded by a water screen, disconnects the
apartments from life outside the tower while
marking the transition from the chaos of the
city to an intimate microcosm. Greenery acts as
a gentle barrier between interior and exterior,
between architecture and city. The gradual
process of privatization that is affecting central
Beirut and its social life is well represented by
Herzog & de Meuron's tower, whose formal
and spatial intentions collide of necessity with
Lebanon's inexorable economic climate. _

herzogdemeuron.com

Thick floor slabs maintain the desired
temperature throughout the day, thus
providing sustainable thermal comfort.

+20

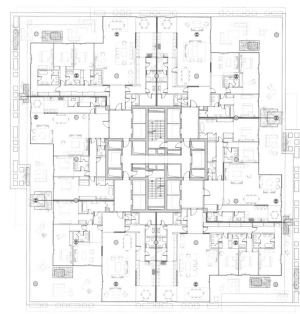

+8

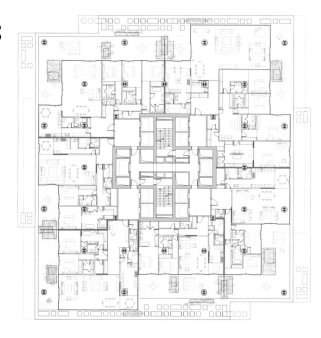

+19

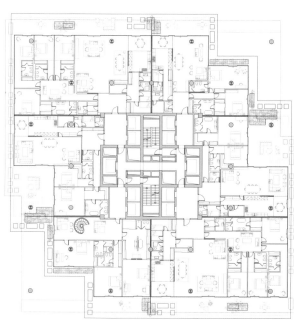

+4

+15

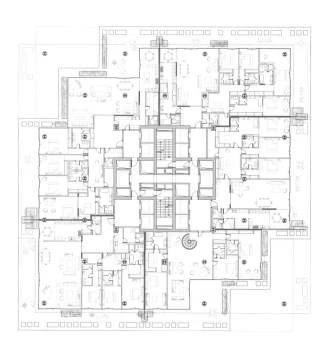

'A podium, decorated with plants and surrounded by a water screen, disconnects the tower from the city'

Section

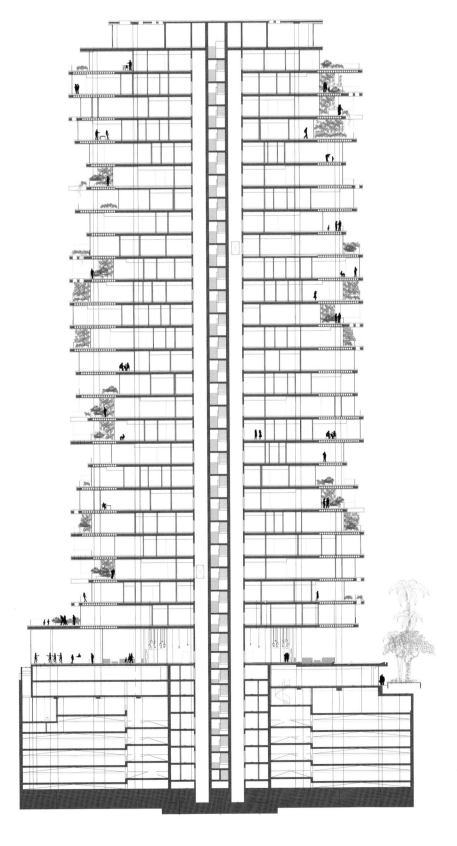

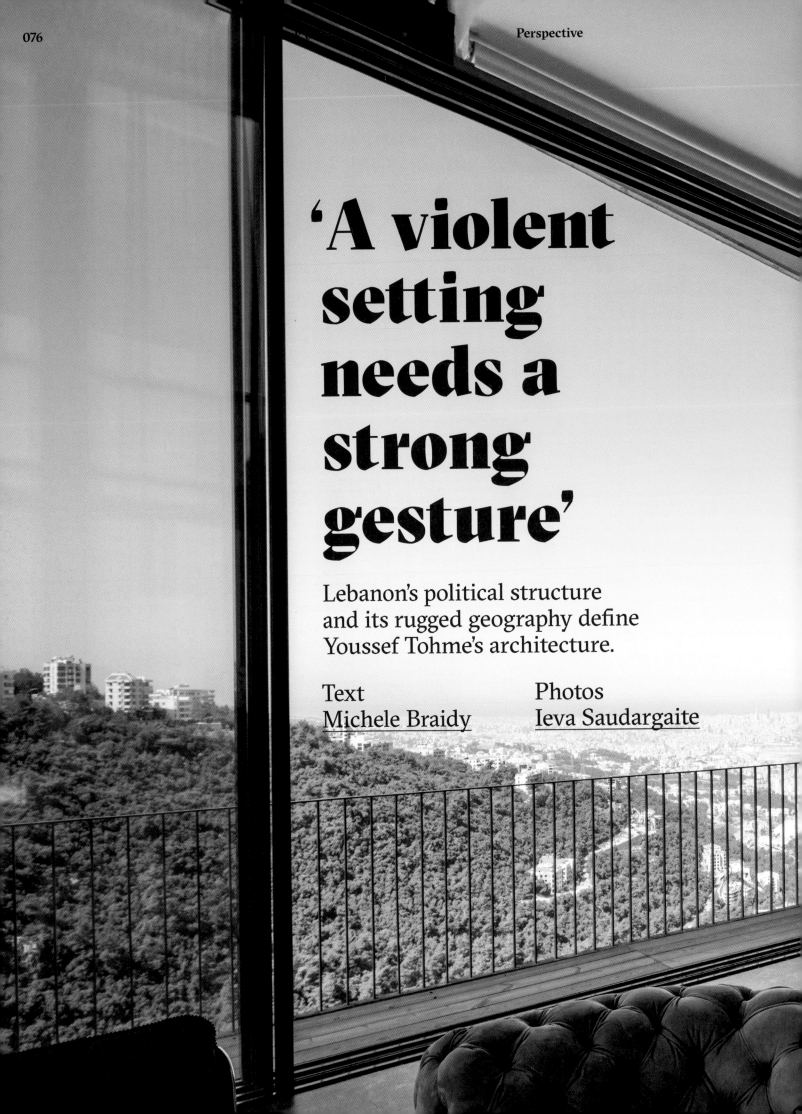

'A violent setting needs a strong gesture'

Lebanon's political structure and its rugged geography define Youssef Tohme's architecture.

Text
Michele Braidy

Photos
Ieva Saudargaite

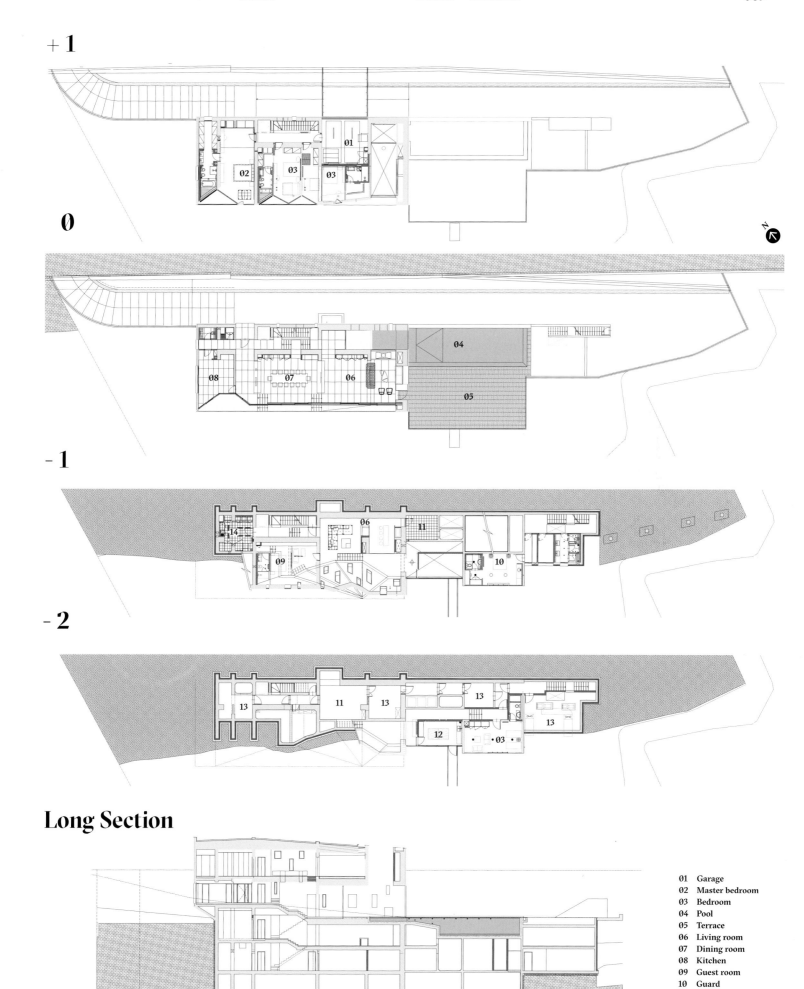

+1

0

-1

-2

Long Section

01 Garage
02 Master bedroom
03 Bedroom
04 Pool
05 Terrace
06 Living room
07 Dining room
08 Kitchen
09 Guest room
10 Guard
11 Storage
12 Atelier
13 Technical room
14 Laundry

The villa's glazed walls and concrete roofs have curved corners.

Villa VR
Ajaltoun — Lebanon — 2017

The two main levels of Villa VR form an entity with
the topography: a sloping site that differs 25 m from its
highest to lowest points. Two expansive white roofs
trace the outlines of both levels, like vast sheets that are
seemingly insubstantial yet solid. Made from prestressed
concrete, they take the material to the limits of its
flexibility. From within, the roof appears to split and
crack, letting natural light enter through the openings.

'<u>I</u> <u>don't</u> have a <u>relationship</u> <u>with nature</u>

Jimenez Lai of Bureau Spectacular about
Laugier's Primitive Hut, page 100

<u>My nature is</u> <u>consumerism</u>'

A School with

Rooftop greenhouses will be a hands-on learning centre for students to grow vegetables and plants.

a View

C.F. Møller's Copenhagen International School is a pioneer in an industrial-transformation zone.

Text
Terri Peters

Photos
Adam Mørk

Copenhagen

International School (CIS), designed by C.F. Møller, assumes a striking pose in Nordhavn, the Danish capital's new waterfront district. At first sight, the complex appears to be wrapped in shimmering blue-green sequins which are, in fact, solar cells. They cover an area of about 6,000 m², making the school one of the largest building-integrated solar-power plants in Denmark, producing about 300 MWh annually – or approximately half the school's electricity consumption.

The school was formerly located in a posh residential suburb in the northern part of the city. In its latest guise, CIS is one of the first completed projects in a large industrial-transformation zone that is based on a master plan for a mixed-use neighbourhood that will eventually be served by public transport. The plan, created by COBE Architects, includes offices and a range of high- and low-rise housing. The site offered the school the learning space and outdoor areas that were needed to double the student population to 1,200 pupils, ages five through 18. It exemplifies the school's ambition to connect to its immediate environment and to the wider community. Architect Mads Mandrup Hansen, involved in the project since the beginning, recalls the day

The new site offered the school the space needed to double its student population.

Jimenez Lai.

Sitting

roughly 4 m above a concrete floor on the roof of an 'indoor treehouse' that has no railings and is absolutely not up to code, I take the opportunity to meditate on the state of healthcare in the US and to worry. Next to me, Jimenez Lai, founder of LA architecture studio Bureau Spectacular and creator of the perilous situation we're in, casually dangles his feet off the edge and talks passionately about everything at once: the 2016 presidential election, elections worldwide, 18th-century architecture critic and philosopher Marc-Antoine Laugier, Le Corbusier, Rem Koolhaas and Home Depot aesthetics. All these topics have a symbolic place at the literal (built-in) table of Another Primitive Hut, the project we're using as a seat and a reference to Laugier's ideas about the relationship between architecture and nature. 'I don't have a relationship with nature,' Lai laughs. 'My nature is consumerism.'

Like all Bureau Spectacular projects, Another Primitive Hut adheres to the motto that architecture should be practised through 'the contemplation of art, history, politics, sociology, linguistics, mathematics, graphic design, technology and storytelling'. And, in the tradition of acronymic architecture firms, Bureau Spectacular fully accepts the possibility that its B.S. monogrammed stationery could indicate a message writ upon bullshit. That's part of 'the contemplation', I'm told, and an example of the outfit's sense of humour. 'Have you read philosopher Harry G. Frankfurt's "On Bullshit"?' Lai asks.

Before getting an official Los Angeles zip code in 2015, Bureau Spectacular was a nomadic firm founded in 2008 by Lai, whose 'cool' reputation preceded his arrival: he'd worked for OMA, lived and worked at Taliesin West, resided in an Atelier van Lieshout shipping container in Rotterdam and authored several books, including 'architectural graphic novel' *Citizens of No Place*, a collection of stories on architecture and urbanism that went on to develop a cult following. Initially, the move to Los Angeles left Lai financially broke but creatively validated, as he found steady clients and progressed to bigger, and built, projects.

In 2016 Bureau Spectacular saw the realization of two important works. At the Coachella Valley Music and Arts Festival, B.S. erected *The Tower of Twelve Stories*, a bright-white, 16-m-high 'fictional apartment building' on stilts. The architects stacked 12 cartoon-like

bubbles for unscripted retreat and left the façade – Chekov's fourth wall – open for public viewing. Inhabitants of the 'apartments' were also in plain sight, exposed to visitors as well as to the elements, making the installation both an elevated den of privacy and another stage for performance.

Pragmatically, *The Tower of Twelve Stories* is also a canopy, providing shade in the desert. No less pragmatically, it references Leonard Cohen's 'Tower of Song', particularly the lyrics: 'I said to Hank Williams, how lonely does it get? Hank Williams hasn't answered yet. But I can hear him coughing, all night long. A hundred floors above me, in the tower of song.' What's more, the installation reflects Louis Sullivan's ideas about 20th-century skyscrapers, while nodding to a painting by Magritte, an essay by Rem Koolhaas and Lai's own architectural comics. Insisting that storytelling and communication are inherent to his profession, Lai says *The Tower of Twelve Stories* 'only becomes real when people populate it'.

The second 2016 milestone for B.S. was the completion of a retail project for fashion brand Frankie. At the downtown LA flagship store, Bureau Spectacular introduced a flexible interior, in which an 8.5-m-long, 2.4-m-high white staircase, or 'bleacher', serves as seating during screenings and events. Easily taken apart, the unit divides into nine modules on wheels that function as fitting rooms, storage space and displays of various heights. Lai calls the modular element 'super-furniture', which he defines as 'a structure too small to be a building but too large to be simply a piece of furniture'.

In its first two months, Frankie changed the interior layout at least three times. Although it's got all the requisites of retail show-and-tell, the design is most notable for its effortless mood swings, its seamless transition between scenes. Not surprisingly, the brief for Frankie was less about material and more about soul. Lai and Frankie founder Kevin Chen made the films of Jean-Luc Godard their reference point. Bureau Spectacular hit the brick exterior with a geometric black-and-white graphic, drawing three-dimensional shadows across the shop's façade. A degree in French New Wave isn't required to recognize the cinematic influence. But B.S. doesn't value the perfectly composed film still as much as the process of editing and reinvention, the ability for people and spaces to continuously change one another. >

'I don't have a relationship with nature. My nature is consumerism'

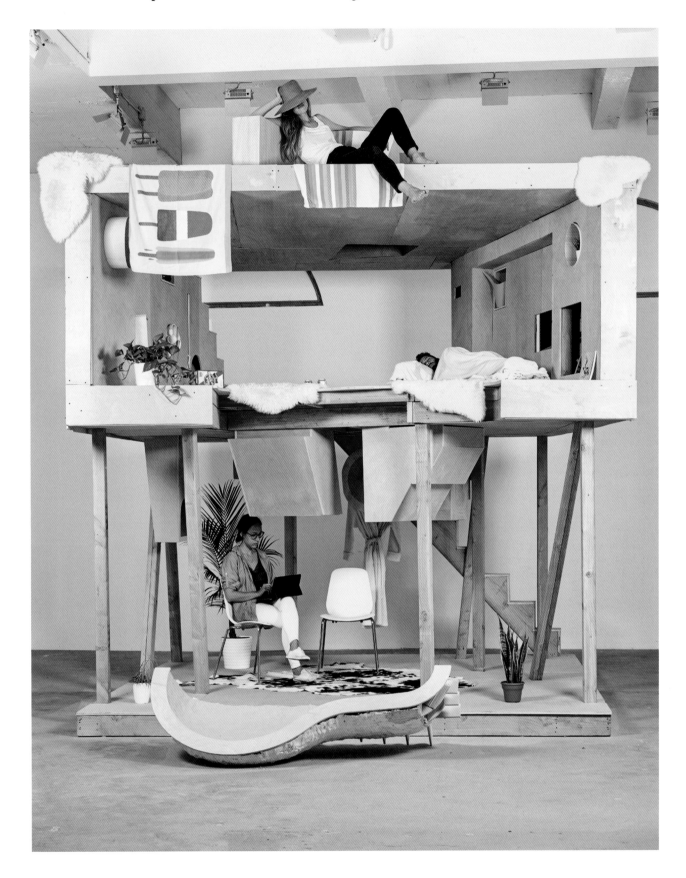

Another Primitive Hut
Los Angeles — USA — 2016

Another Primitive Hut is a chamber that welcomes friends and
family to enter a domestic environment. It is a place for social
gatherings, whether or not anyone wants to gather any more. It
is a project that asks us to consider what it means to be a human
at this stage in history and to imagine the chapters still to come.

Lai takes pleasure in defying the restrictions and permanence of architecture. Back at Another Primitive Hut, we carefully (very carefully) make our way down the treehouse, as Lai complains that 'in LA – as in many places around the world – it's bureaucracy that builds architecture, not architects. The only place to do something actually free is inside buildings.'

The treehouse is a free zone without a façade, a three-storey shelter within a shelter. It once served as a living room, dining room and gathering space for Bureau Spectacular, back when it lived in B.S.'s downtown studio. 'I've served lunch to 12 people on its roof,' says Lai. 'Every Tuesday I cook for the office, and this was a space where we could eat together. There's something primal about sharing food and sharing ideas – that's when we accidentally talk about something social that's related to our work and make it better.'

Like most free spirits, the treehouse didn't get on with Lai's landlord, who kicked it out for being a liability. Another Primitive Hut now lives a solitary life in a storage space by the ocean. Lai hopes its lonely home is temporary. Exemplary of a Bureau Spectacular project, the treehouse is an extrovert, getting its energy from people. Another Primitive Hut is also an appropriate symbol for the inevitable conflict between freedom and constraint that marks Bureau Spectacular's transformation from designers on paper to practising architects. As we leave the ocean and drive downtown to company headquarters, Lai tells me about his interest in Toyo Ito's trajectory, particularly those eight years between Ito opening shop under the pseudonym Urbot (Urban Robot) and his rebaptism as Toyo Ito & Associates, as he went from 'publications, exhibitions and theoretical work to getting "real" jobs'.

Lai thinks of Bureau Spectacular as a 'band that occasionally changes drummers'.

His partner, architect Joanna Grant, became an integral part of the band when she joined in 2013, and in 2014 she and Lai designed the Taiwan pavilion at the Venice Architecture Biennale. At present, they work with three additional people at the office, and while B.S. 'responds to the people who work here at any given time', Lai insists on maintaining the firm's core character, a subject that will take us back to Toyo Ito in due time – storytelling, remember?

The downtown studio is an industrial loft, seven storeys above a lively urban stretch, where the clucks of chickens compete with the growls of people and cars. Inside, we walk past a long table, gorgeously crammed with models and notes for current projects, among which an event design for Redcat, a contemporary arts centre in LA; *Insideoutsidebetweenbeyond*, an installation for the San Francisco Museum of Modern Art; and a proposal for Pool Party, a splish-splash urban oasis for MoMA PS1 in New York City.

From the studio, Lai and I walk up to the roof of the building, which overlooks the city below, and he returns to Toyo Ito's dramatic eight-year-long studio metamorphosis. Lai is on year seven of B.S. and 'if our studio didn't transform with time, I would think of it as a problem'. Change is part of Bureau Spectacular's DNA, and it's also part of the mnemonic coat of arms that Lai designed for his organization: the black queen of the game of chess next to a white heart within a black diamond. The queen, signifying the most desirable chess piece for its ability to move undeterred is 'our reminder not to give up and not to die', he says. The heart in a diamond is 'to remember to stay soft on the inside'. _

bureau-spectacular.net

The 16-m-high installation is open at the front, exposing a stack of cartoonish 'bubbles' that function as apartments.

Office KGDVS's Solo House exemplifies an ongoing shift towards exceptionality in contemporary architecture.

Text
Rafael Gómez-Moriana

Photos
Bas Princen

The roof features water tanks and generators, designed as sculptural objects. Energy is provided by photovoltaic cells.

Solo

Houses is the name of a project that's intended to include more than a dozen villas designed by different architects. The location is a mountainous region in northeast Spain, not far from the border with Catalonia and about three hours from Barcelona by car. If you're looking for 'the middle of nowhere', this is the place to be. So far, two Solo Houses have been completed, the first in 2013 by Chilean studio Pezo Von Ellrichshausen and the second a contribution by Belgian firm Office Kersten Geers David Van Severen (KGDVS). In addition to these two firms, other participants are Sou Fujimoto, Johnston Marklee, Christ & Gantenbein, Didier Faustino, Studio Mumbai, Anne Holtrop, Barozzi Veiga, Rintala Eggerston, MOS, Go Hasegawa, Kühn Malvezzi, Tatiana Bilbao, TNA, Smiljan Radi and Bas Smets.

Solo Houses are nothing like the pseudo-Spanish holiday homes we know from tourist brochures and travel blogs. These more conceptual villas are, according to the literature, 'an ongoing project of contemporary small resort prototypes'. The venture is the brainchild of Christian Bourdais, a French property developer who, together with art producer Eva Albarran, is also responsible for the Solo Gallery in Paris, a space dedicated to 'architects who display a truly artistic approach in their work'. Solo claims to be 'the first contemporary art gallery to exhibit works of architects in their own right'.

The conflation of private property development and modern art is as old as urban gentrification, which inevitably follows the moves of 'pioneering' artists, but the sparsely populated wilderness chosen for Solo Houses is far away from artists' lofts and trendy cafés. The closest recent precedent for this kind of development is probably the failed Ordos 100 venture in China, planned by Ai Wei Wei and curated by Herzog & de Meuron, but Ordos was promoted as a design-driven development meant to serve a new Chinese metropolis badly in need of some cachet. Solo Houses is more modest in scale, slower in progress and, as the name suggests, entirely on its own.

Remarkably, the Spanish project is by a private developer who seems genuinely passionate about art and architecture and not on one who's simply eager to give the project an artistic mantle. As such, it says something about the kind of atypical context in which architecture is encouraged to thrive relatively unencumbered by convention, legislation or market demand. Serious architecture is increasingly forced to seek refuge under the institutional umbrella of serious art in order to be taken 'seriously'. In the process, it becomes the stuff of private and public collectors, galleries, museums, biennials and curated exhibitions – architecture for the art world more than the real world.

Furthermore, as a series of 'resort prototypes' presumably meant as temporary retreats rather than year-round homes, Solo Houses exemplifies the ongoing shift in architecture towards exceptionality, leisure time and the kinds of 'experiences' that social networks entice us to share online. Since the end of modernism, we've come to know that *haute* architecture is not something most people would choose to reside in permanently. But we have also discovered, in turn, that this kind of architecture is accepted more when it is something to visit or reside in temporarily, in which case it is seen as a fun experience. If 'social housing' was an architectural mantra in the early 20th-century, that of the 21st century would clearly have to be 'funhouses'.

The latest Solo House – rather ironically titled Solo Office – is indeed a lot of fun. To begin with, it's round. In fact, it's a sprawling, circular loop that offers panoramic views from its hilltop site, as it embraces and domesticates a piece of the comprehensive project's back of beyond. Essentially, Solo Office is a covered 4.5-m-wide walkway that encompasses enclosed areas – or what the architects call 'houses' – that function as living, cooking and sleeping quarters. The circular roof rests on four straight rows of steel columns that form a square with chamfered corners. The spaces – or 'houses' – between columns and perimeter leave large parts of the walkway unprogrammed and ready for all types of planned and unplanned use. They come in handy at big cocktail parties, for instance, and are great for lounging around in. Sliding walls suspended from rails that run without interruption along the edge of the roof allow each 'house' to open to the outside; the same walls thus shelter the 'free spaces' from wind, rain, prying eyes – or cameras. A swimming pool within the wide round courtyard looks quite 'natural' by virtue of its subtly undulating edge and irregularly formed steps where it meets the untouched landscape. A gravel path connects the pool steps with the looped walkway, making this an ideal villa for barefoot masochists.

Although Solo Office's doughnut-shaped design recalls that of several projects attempting to justify circularity on the grounds of functionality – among which Apple Corporation's nearly completed Spaceship >

'Contact with nature has always been

The Solo House designed by Office KGDVS is approximately 300 m away from the first Solo House, designed by Pezo Von Ellrichshausen and completed in 2013.

what villas are about'

The architects wanted to make 'as little house as possible' so that occupants could live 'without boundaries between the house and the nature surrounding it'.

Campus in Cupertino, California, by Norman Foster; OMA's competition entry for the City of Culture of Galicia in Santiago de Compostela, Spain; and the International Centre for Sports Innovation in Cáceres, Spain, by José María Sánchez García – in this case the shape is arbitrary and seemingly conceived purely for the fun of it. Why not, as long as it works? Curiously, the straight lines of an orthogonal building are rarely justified, but the designer of a round building often feels obliged to invent all kinds of pretexts, whereas here in northeast Spain, the architects of a building that dares to combine circles and squares offer no explanation whatsoever.

What you see is pure folly paired with a strict geometry that makes the work highly mathematical and abstract. On one level, it can be seen as a piece of conceptual architecture in the tradition of some of the driest conceptual art ever made. But while a concern for geometry often results in highly solipsistic intellectual exercises removed from

any consideration for the wellbeing of people, this house is *also* very much about enjoyment and pleasure. In that regard, it falls squarely, not to say roundly, within the tradition of the Mediterranean villa, the Ur-prototype of which is Hadrian's Villa near Tivoli, the subject of scholars who have spent centuries trying to make sense of its geometry, never stopping to consider whether it was intended to make sense at all.

Ultimately, Solo Office's looped geometry, operable walls and seemingly neglected courtyard serve no other purpose than to maximize its occupants' close contact with nature and the pleasure this gives them. This has always been what villas are about. In an age in which the word 'nature' increasingly appears between quotation marks – a reference to its portended demise and the proliferation of its artificial simulation – it is reassuring to see that nature-embracing architecture (or is it art?) still has the power to throw us for a loop. –

officekgdvs.com

Large stretches of curtain façade slide along the outer edge of the circle, opening living areas to the outdoors as desired and maximizing the occupants' close contact with nature.

Photo Martina Bjorn

The concrete supporting structure forms
a striking element in the living room.
Photo Jan Steenblock

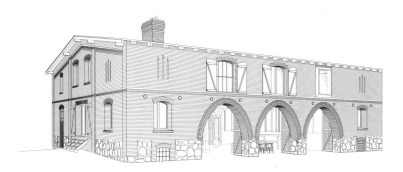

Tenne
Fergitz — Germany — 2014

In a small village in the Uckermark, north of Berlin, a large barn has been converted into a country house with an additional independent apartment. The barn was built 140 years ago in brick with a timber structure. At some point, it was divided into two parts. Thomas Kröger refurbished one half for a young family. The centre of the house is a double-height living room with fireplace. Three major arched openings, which can be closed with large wooden shutters, open to expose the orchard and green expanses beyond. The house is designed so that the unheated great hall is enclosed by a heated body of rooms. In cold seasons, only the smaller and more sociable areas of the house can be used.

The barn has been restored, but with added new features.

When the doors to the garden are open, the hall becomes a covered terrace.

'Old houses often contain so much sensibility and beauty'

The dining room offers a view of the cherry tree orchard.

The terrace overlooks Pinnow Lake.

'I hope our designs don't just show our ideas, but that they also inspire impressions of their own'

Fun

and Games

Giancarlo Mazzanti provided a kindergarten in Barranquilla with a stimulating environment.

Text
Cathelijne Nuijsink

Photos
Rodrigo Dávila

Giancarlo

Mazzanti's latest kindergarten in Barranquilla, in the north of Colombia, is composed of a series of glazed circles and voids and can accommodate up to 175 children between the ages of 3 months and 4 years. The architect explains the philosophy behind the project.

<u>You have designed multiple kindergartens and schools during your career. Can you explain the 'evolution' of this building typology within your portfolio?</u>
GIANCARLO MAZZANTI: For many years we've been researching how school environments have the possibility to generate new forms of behaviour and therefore how new teaching methodologies can work together with

The semi-open concrete façades have deformations that give the impression that huge balls were thrown against them from the inside.
Photo Alfredo Manjarres

different spatial configurations. We believe that school settings themselves can be learning mechanisms. In the first schools we designed, we started working with the idea of using pieces, modules and systems. We projected them as toys that could be assembled and work as open-ended and ever-changing structures.

From there, we developed a line of research whose objectives are to understand the performative capacity of our school projects and the value of games and playfulness in today's social life, criticizing in a way the concept of functionality and how modern buildings were built based only on ideas of efficiency and utility. Each project, then, is an opportunity to ask: What can happen if we

introduce new ways of using space, not only those based on effectiveness and utility? This is why we support ludic activities. Ludic activities are not only instruments to generate new forms of architecture, but are also capable of solving problems and generating fantasies and new ways of using space.

What's the idea behind the type of kindergarten you designed this time, consisting of circular thematic spaces set within an open patio and surrounded by a semi-transparent exterior wall?
The idea was to develop spaces that are visually related but at the same time acoustically separated. Each circle is a classroom that can

be joined to the next one. Curtains allow these areas to be opened or closed, letting kids see and learn from each other. This refers to a strategy of curiosity: if I see what others are doing, it makes me curious and I want to go there too and interact.

So the glazed walls are designed as a kind of interactive device?
Each circle generates reflections that, in my experience, create a sensation similar to being inside a Dan Graham sculpture.

Who runs this kindergarten?
The client is a psychologist who works with a teaching method called *Reggio Emilia* >

developed in the 1940s by Italian educator Loris Malaguzzi, which in my opinion is one of the most fascinating models of exchange and education. The director of the kindergarten, Silvia Pinedo, defined it as 'a space for children', and rather than a simple school it is a cultural and educational centre that interacts with its urban and social context.

<u>How do we see this teaching philosophy reflected in your design?</u>
Transparency, dialogue, expression, freedom, flexibility and movement are characteristics visible in both the educational and architectural project of the centre. Every element of the centre makes it possible to

create connections that become learning experiences. As such, the project moves away from an extreme planning and an inflexible programming of the building, to give users a space to explore, experiment and interact. The resulting environment is, as Malaguzzi has said, the 'third teacher' [the first two being adults and other children]. It is an element of re-creation.

On the other hand, in this kindergarten, teachers act as facilitators. They do not direct, but encourage and support kids to define their interests throughout the process. The micro universe developed by the pedagogical team is, according to the director, a place where nothing is pre-established.

Both the pedagogy and the environment of the kindergarten are grounded on a flexible approach to learning. Just like the lives of the girls and boys, this is a place open to continuous transformation.

<u>It seems you have spent quite some time designing the concrete façade. What is the idea behind the façade detailing?</u>
The façade is a thermal membrane that is deformed as if it was hit by balls from inside the school. It works as a brise-soleil that protects the interior from the intense Caribbean sun. At the same time, it allows air to flow through the façade, which helps to improve the climatic conditions inside.

Through the Looking Glass

Three works of art by Doug Aitken consider modern life through modern architecture.

Text
Katya Tylevich

large sign prohibits all dogs, so the number of Yorkies on site must mean the spirit of protest is alive and well in Southern California. This is a project that literally reflects its context, and right now the composure of *Mirage*, by artist Doug Aitken, is challenged by the unpredictability of its visitors and their contraband. Another sign implores visitors to refrain from taking photographs or videos. It is blatantly disregarded. Well, isn't this a tidy allegory for the dilemmas of architecture? Places for living expose the chasm between intentions and inhabitants. 'Wow, I've never seen anything like this before,' says a stranger in a Hawaiian-print shirt. Actually, sir, you have.

At face value, *Mirage*, part of temporary art exhibition Desert X, is a suburban ranch house made of reflective glass and sited on a residential desert hillside in Palm Springs. Its outline is purposely generic and familiar, reminiscent of the cookie-cutter post-war American home (and the American Dream, of course). The soul of *Mirage* is a mirror of your own projections. Walking within or around the 'house', you see, at various points, an image of yourself, multiple versions of yourself or of someone else, the naked desert, a rattlesnake, or a stunning gridded vista of urban sprawl in the valley below. Visitors are confronted with dizzying reflections, which are punctuated by views through deliberately placed windows. Sometimes it's difficult to tell whether you are looking at 'reality' or through the looking glass.

As a private experience, *Mirage* is a meditation on the kind of life prescribed by a structure like this. The personal response may be a memory, an aspiration, or revulsion. Were it not for the reflection of moving bodies on its exterior, *Mirage* would camouflage itself into its environment, would seem immaterial, illusive – not unlike the utopian ideas that, among other less noble intentions, fuelled the spread of suburban neighbourhoods in the post-war United States. Here, bodies in motion disrupt all moments of solipsism; they walk into frame and alter the meaning of the scene. The light changes, as does the position of the sun, the clouds, the weather, the mood. As a 'clean' installation, *Mirage* gives the false impression of serenity, when it is in fact constantly disturbed.

The structure both absorbs and reflects the landscape around it.
Photo Dakota Higgins / courtesy of the artist and Desert X

Mirage
Desert Palisades — Palm Springs — USA — 2017

Mirage is an installation that is part of contemporary art festival Desert X. It presents a continually changing encounter in which subject and object, inside and outside, are in constant flux. Every available surface of the ranch-style structure is clad in mirrored surfaces. As *Mirage* pulls the landscape in and reflects it out, this classic one-storey suburban house becomes a framing device, a perceptual echo chamber endlessly bouncing between the dream of nature as a pure uninhabited state and the pursuit of its conquest.

Like all works of architecture, even those green ones with the smallest of footprints, *Mirage* is an intrusion upon nature. It is cognizant of its attempts at discretion, even as it is a foreign object in a prehistoric landscape. As a result, *Mirage* comments on the expertly branded modern development in which it is currently located. This is a gated community, within which *Mirage* is both an advertisement (life as an impeccably produced work of art) and a subversion. After all, *Mirage* actively attracts outsiders to a neighbourhood that has all the subtlety of a 'keep out' notice. To get to *Mirage*, you need to pass a security roundabout. The public art installation is a trespasser on both the artificial (social) and natural environment. So, then, is the viewer, who might feel a little >

Mirage will be open to visitors until the end of October.
Photo Lance Gerber / courtesy of the artist and Desert X

Underwater Pavilions **is an art installation off the California coast near Catalina Island, south of Los Angeles.**
Photos Doug Aitken Workshop / courtesy of the artist, Parley for the Oceans, and MOCA Los Angeles

Underwater Pavilions
Avalon — USA — 2016

Underwater Pavilions consists of three temporary underwater sculptures moored to the ocean floor. Geometric in design, they create living environments that reflect and refract light, opening a portal that physically connects the viewer to the expanse of the ocean. By merging the language of contemporary architecture, land art and ocean awareness, *Underwater Pavilions* becomes a living work of art within a vibrant ecosystem.

defensive about the boundaries between private and public that are reinforced by architecture.

A recurring characteristic of Aitken's work is its nomadism. Not only does the viewer travel to see works like *Mirage*; the work itself is a rolling stone. Aitken plans to move *Mirage* in the near future, possibly to Taliesin West – Frank Lloyd Wright's 'winter home' in Scottsdale, Arizona – where it will reflect an entirely different set of truths, aspirations, tensions and failures. In the past year, Aitken has inadvertently created a trilogy of works that evoke tropes of modern architecture as symbols for modern life. They invite a mutual transformation. The works change in response to their environments, and viewers change in response to the works.

In June, Aitken's project *The Garden* opened in Aarhus, Denmark, as part of the ARoS Triennial. Like *Mirage*, *The Garden* also highlights tensions inherent within 'generic' symbols of modernism. This time, the symbol is a transparent glass box, not exactly Miesian but with a Miesian aftertaste.

To access *The Garden*, you enter one of several anonymous warehouses at the end of a dock. Once inside, confronted by darkness, you make your way through a jungle of artificially fabricated 'organic' nature, through the oxygen and humidity it emits, and towards a glowing geometric construction in the distance. The interior of this rectangular glass structure is outfitted with minimalist necessities of domestic life – namely, modern living-room

furniture and decor. You experience the work as both subject and surveyor. Visitors inhabit the structure, which is composed of thick bulletproof glass, one at a time. Each has permission to obliterate and violently destroy the trappings of modern life inside, should this prove desirable. People outside the glazed walls can watch. Aitken's project description calls the resulting frenzy a 'release of and against the modern environment. Does it somehow go without saying that 'the modern environment' is a source of emotional repression? That it's satisfying to smash its pretty little ideas?

Both *Mirage* and *The Garden* demonstrate a strained relationship between the regulatory idealism of modern structures and the fragmented, nonlinear, explosive ways

The geometric structures of mirror and rock are accessible only to marine life and to scuba divers.
Photo Patrick T. Fallon / courtesy of the artist, Parley for the Oceans and MOCA Los Angeles

in which we actually live our lives. *The Garden*, of course, invites a physical fragmentation – an eruption – of interior life. When I meet Aitken in his Venice, California, studio, I ask if the two works are meant as a critique of modern architecture – perhaps a critique of the unrealistic narrative of health and integrated living that modern architecture imposes on an otherwise chaotic existence. Aitken doesn't want to use the c-word, instead describing his intention to 'break down' such narratives, to 'crack them open' and allow people to 'enter' their shambles.

'When a person enters a work like that, they are inescapably – one to one – living in real time with their surroundings.' The relationship between person and structure

is levelled; the inhabitant somehow has greater power over the architecture through manipulation or destruction rather than everyday use or – God forbid – simple viewership. Aitken wants to make a person a physical subject of these works, not just a witness or even a participant. The spontaneity of relationships between visitors and art installations is an exaggeration of the everyday power struggle between designed aspiration and sloppy actuality. Aitken designs a controlled environment for loss of control.

Last December, Aitken placed three large geometric structures underwater, in the Pacific Ocean off the California coast near Catalina Island. The project was realized with help from Parley, an organization for

the protection of oceans. The *Underwater Pavilions* are accessible only to marine life and scuba-certified humans. They are composed of glass mirrors and 'hand-carved composite designed to foster marine growth with a goal of "interactivity"'. Like *Mirage*, the *Pavilions* reflect their surroundings. They also become their surroundings – are overrun by them, resembling ruins of modern civilization.

Adhering to Aitken's interest in nomadism, the *Pavilions* will eventually 'migrate' (be transported) to other bodies of water. When they move, the new life that colonized these man-made habitats will be professionally removed and left in the waters. This is a piece that fosters new growth while reminding us of loss and displacement. >

Difficult not to think of the dying Great Barrier Reef, irreversibly wrecked by climate change. Strange, somehow, that Aitken's man-made structures actually contribute to the regrowth of an ecosystem. This is deliberate, of course, and in conflict with expectation. Like *Mirage* and *The Garden*, the *Pavilions* are a hallucination that one can physically touch.

'The first time I dove the *Underwater Pavilions*, it was wintertime, the ocean was cold and the sky was stormy,' Aitken tells me. 'I became aware that I was breathing air in a place in which I shouldn't be able to breathe. All of a sudden, I was seeing these shining, geometric shapes in the distance. I moved towards them in slow motion, while horizontal, through space with seemingly no gravity. No

longer on terra firma, I experienced the shock of the new – a disturbance of what I know, thrust into a very unfamiliar condition.'

Of the three works, *Underwater Pavilions* most forcibly demonstrates a break with designed navigation, by suspending normal human movement and 'letting go'. These three pieces are built upon architectural metaphor: they are an outward representation of modern structures, but all three have the quality of being or becoming immaterial. Their minimalist, perfectionist execution exists solely for the purposeful loss of perfection – for overgrowth, for destruction. They are not an admonishment of the architecture they represent but an observation of its limitations in the face of the living organisms around and within them.

'It's a perverse relationship,' says Aitken. 'I try to make everything perfect but am aware that in a few hours or days these pieces will be transformed completely beyond recognition. I can't make the work climate-controlled,' he laughs. 'I like the idea of containers of energy and disruption, of continual changing, changing, changing.' —
dougaitkenworkshop.com

'I like the idea

The Garden
Aarhus — Denmark — 2017

The first ARoS Triennial, entitled *The Garden – End of Times; Beginning of Times*, includes Aitken's interactive art installation, which embraces the dichotomy between natural and man-made environments. The piece is based on therapeutic 'anger rooms', in which participants are invited to destroy their surroundings.

Images Doug Aitken Workshop / courtesy of the artist and ARoS Aarhus Kunstmuseum

The installation at the opening of the ARoS Triennial.

Renderings showing a visitor of *The Garden* at work.

# of containers of energy and disruption'

Teaching Space

Aires Mateus built a Faculty of Architecture that allows freedom of appropriation.

Text
Ana Martins

Photos
Tim Van de Velde

Outstanding

buildings don't have to be the result of towering funds, lavish materials or an exhaustive planning of functions and spaces. These are some of the lessons that can be learnt from the new Faculty of Architecture in Tournai, designed by Portuguese studio Aires Mateus and inaugurated in March this year.

Lisbon-based architects and brothers Manuel and Francisco Aires Mateus won a competition launched by the Université Catholique de Louvain (UCL) in 2013 for the construction of a new campus for its Faculty of Architecture. The programme saw the move of the school from Tournai's periphery to a block in the centre of one of Belgium's oldest cities.

Built with a strict budget of 4 million euros, the 7000-m² complex that includes a library, an auditorium, workshops, classrooms and administrative spaces, is the outcome of 'a spartan project'. As we discuss the project, Manuel Aires Mateus explains how this austerity was welcomed as a liberating challenge in the design process and, ultimately, made the school what it is today.

How specific was UCL's brief for the competition?
MANUEL AIRES MATEUS: There was something very interesting about this competition: it imposed very few things. There was the site, a 6,000-m² block, where only one of the pre-existing buildings had to

be preserved: an old convent, later converted into a hospital. Other than that there were two limitations: time and money. Our proposal involved taking advantage of these very limits.

How so?
In order to make the construction as expeditious and economic as possible, we decided to keep, besides the old convent, two industrial buildings. Then, from the moment that all of the other existing architecture was taken out of the equation, a single gesture revealed itself: a building that would unite all of the different elements, both vertically and horizontally; draw the public spaces; and establish a relationship with the manifold surroundings. This was our first reaction to the project, and it remained more or less the same until the end.

What aspects of this first approach changed?
In the initial programme, the new building was a huge container, inhabited by architectural archetypes that served different functions. Then, as we felt the need to evoke a space that was part of the school's identity, these forms were pushed to the limits of the building and transformed into its doors, windows and passageways, and the space became an empty foyer. Just as in the old school, the students now have a multifunctional space that can be used for anything from exhibitions to

conferences, and, more importantly, as a day-to-day meeting place. This way, the foyer not only solves all of the building's problems in terms of visual and physical connections, but becomes the heart of the new school.

The school sits in a block that is bordered by an industrial area on one side and a residential street on the other. How did you integrate the building into two such disparate environments?
We designed each exterior shape so that all parts of the building would be related to one another, as well as to the different scales of the surroundings. For instance, the main entrance, with its imposing portico, faces the industrial area, while the back entrance uses the scale and details of the secondary, residential street. This connection is also established physically. The idea is that the building is a public crossing in the city, it's open and everyone can go through. I don't know how much that will happen, but that's our intention. In fact, the central garden is imagined as a public space.

What informed your choice of colour for the new building?
Since we couldn't use the red brick and *pierre bleue* of the exisiting structures, we wanted to draw quality from them. So, we looked for a colour that would not only emphasize these materials, but take advantage of their properties. We chose this specific grey cement-based cladding, which we used both in the exterior and the interior, from a thousand variations of the colour, but it was always grey, we never thought it could be any other colour.

The entire process, from project execution until the school was inaugurated in March, took less than three years. What contributed to this?
First and foremost, there was a pressing necessity to get it done very quickly: the school had to leave its previous location on a set date.

Another factor is that we presented the proposal with Tradeco, a Belgian construction firm. Together, we studied what would be the quickest, easiest and most effective construction methods. We used a lot of prefabrication, for instance. So, even though there was a more lengthy part of the process that had to do with approvals and politics, from the moment everything was approved, the assembly was very swift.

Were there any major issues you had to circumvent arising from the phase of approvals? >

The central garden is meant to be a public space.

The back entrance is adjusted to
the scale of the residential street.

I soon found myself in a somewhat bizarre cycle of working over the year. This is going to sound ludicrously random: in the spring, I need to fantasize – or dream, which I have done frequently – of what I want to talk about the following fall. I trust my intuition, because I find that quite often even in a topic that sound quite odd, I have conjured it out of the air – the same air that other people breathe. Normally you would think, for example, this year's topic of 'miracles' would be esoteric and weird – especially in an architecture school – and yet the moment I start saying it people seem to not just approve of it, but also get it and get why I want to think about this strange thing now. A past topic was 'angels', which had the same eerie feeling; especially if you consider the rise of the digital – as angels were a mode of communication, inhabiting a pre-modern cyberspace. Another topic for a series was the 'ugly', which was really about having a quasi-positive attitude towards the ugly.

Fortunately, nobody at the AA questions the relevance of these topics to contemporary architecture. Once I think of the topic, I get into the London Library and start working bibliographically, assembling things that I think I must read, and by the end of the summer I have a list of lecture titles. Then I spend the week before a lecture thinking about it all the time that I can – which is much more than you think, because when you work as I do, you are never not-working. It may be a question of thinking out an argument, it may be just thinking of words. I make it an internal rule to make sure that I have worked it out in my mind sufficiently, so that when I deliver the lecture I don't need notes, but I'm relying on a text that's in my head. Perhaps the reason I do not use a word processor is because, in a sense, I am one.

Admittedly, you read more than most people do.
The crude truth is that I am addicted to reading: it shows all the characteristics of an addiction. If I go long enough without reading I start wondering what on earth life is for. The purpose in life, I think, is a book. Even if you don't write books, it doesn't matter – you are writing all the time. You could call it other things – like reflection – but that term lacks a certain brutal crudity. Indeed, people would say that it is what removes you from existence because I am not usually interested in what you're supposed to be interested in, what you're seeing or being at, but I am interested in the odd bits of discussion.

Could you give an example?
The kind of thing I have been interested in for a while is the alternative history of the house. I saw that someone just designed a house in Bel-Air for half a billion dollars; I looked at it

'The role of theory is to get non-architectural discourse off the back of architecture'

Mark Cousins Recommends

Peter Brown, *Through the Eye of a Needle: Wealth, the Fall of Rome, and the Making of Christianity in the West, 350-550 AD*, Princeton University Press, Princeton, 2012

Roland Barthes, *Michelet par lui-même*, Éditions du Seuil, Paris, 1954

Jean-Pierre Vernant and Pierre Vidal-Naquet, *Myth and Tragedy in Ancient Greece*, Zone Books, New York, 1988

Georges Canguilhem, *The Normal and the Pathological*, Zone Books, New York, 1991

very carefully, the pictures and the drawings, and I kept trying to figure out what exactly is it. There is no point in calling it a palace, which is what social historians might call it. I realized that what it is, is a hotel. And the relation of the quasi-official 'hotel' with what you may call 'the domestic' is getting stronger and stronger. It's also not reckless to say that it is really the logo of Donald Trump. Trump *is* a hotel, and not just because he trades in them, but because his mind is like a hotel; his whole take on existence is that of a hotel. Take a few characteristics of the hotel. The hotel, as it greets us, has no past. It lives in a continuous present, temporarily marked by workers' shifts, while the past is something that is 'cleaned up' and thrown away every morning. The preparation of a room, where a guest will exist (for a lack of a better term) is in a space that has been industrially cleansed of the past. The notepaper is new, the scribbling pad has not been written on, nobody has ever been here, or rather they have vanished into the confidentiality of the hotel's billing archive. Something of the same is true for Trump's mind: a hotel manager finds it easy to say, in refuting an argument – 'but that was yesterday'. It's undoubtedly a formulation that Trump will be using often as president.

Lastly, what would you say you have learned from most?
I worked at the Warburg Institute, which had the strangest organization I have ever seen. There were four stories to the library: 'Word', 'Image', 'Orientation' and 'Action'. So the library has a philosophical frame to it that is very carefully and beautifully orchestrated by the librarian. Its classification system is unbelievable – it's at the opposite end of the DOI [Digital Object Identifier] system. The classification system is, basically, by intuition as to what is significant. Some sections are amazing, showcasing 'the left hand' next to 'the bad prince'. In a longstanding row with the university, who kept trying to submit and subject the library to the DOI system, the university lost. Even when they got American consultants from the DOI System, they said that they wouldn't know how to classify at least 30 per cent of the books, they just won't fit; it is the fitting of the library-that-won't-fit. It is where you learn that adjacency can be inspiring; it is a library that compels you to be browsing all the time. Actually, if you can't find a book on the specific floor, it often works three-dimensionally: you can go down or up and look at the same place, and you will probably find what you were looking for. This is a library that celebrates the unexpected – which turns out to be just the thing you needed. ⎯

a strong cultural dimension to the bathroom and we want to communicate that,' says Meiré. 'A bathroom is usually very private; everything happens behind closed doors. It's also about sexuality and ageing. This is culturally relevant.'

The commission for Dornbracht wasn't Neri&Hu's first collaboration with a sanitary wares manufacturer. 'We designed our first bathtub, which was launched in Milan during the past Salone, for Agape,' says Lyndon Neri. For Dornbracht, Neri&Hu was looking for 'a sense of the domestic ritual within bathing spaces'. The designers came up with a beautiful concrete structure, where the arched ceilings and shallow pond recall Le Corbusier's Legislative Assembly in Chandigarh, India. Furthermore, they used a lot of marble and combined both wall- and deck-mounted taps with one brass washing basin. Part of the ceiling is open, to give the space the characteristics of a courtyard.

Rafael de Cárdenas made multiple designs, of which one had a plan with strongly curved walls. 'We were encouraged to design an environment with a high fantasy quotient,' says De Cárdenas. 'Yet it was also meant to reflect the notion of a "transitional style", which is about the juxtaposition of the traditional and the contemporary, and which initially informed the design of the fittings. So, for example, we gave a prominent place to brick masonry, a consummately traditional practice, but we inflected it with a distinctly non-traditional coursing to break up the gravity of the walls and infuse the classical with a sense of contemporaneity.' The design by De Cárdenas has earthly colours and soft, round shapes. The taps are affixed to a cubistic piece of bathroom furniture made of different, dark coloured materials, like Corian and smoked glass.

Although initially there were no plans to actually realize the designs, Meiré doesn't exclude that from happening – 'for something like a fair stand'. After the renderings were done, two mock-ups were built for the photoshoot. Some of the materials in those were real, and others were imitated and then refined in Photoshop. 'So the pictures are a cross-over,' says Meiré. 'For now, it's about the imagery.' The images were then turned into trailers that can be seen on social media, such as facebook.com/dornbracht. In order to stimulate a discourse about transitional style in progressive interiors, Dornbracht also created the hashtag #createanewbalance.

dornbracht.com

Based on the conceptual approaches of Neri&Hu, Vaia in matte platinum is central within the bathroom architecture.
Photo <u>Thomas Popinger</u>

The bathroom architecture for the matte dark platinum Vaia ties in with the central elements of Rafael de Cárdenas's design, and also with the range of finishes and colours outlined in the material collage.
Photo <u>Thomas Popinger</u>

Neri&Hu's architectural concept focuses on the atrium.

Exit
Mark 70
Oct — Nov 2017

Photo *Marco Cappelletti*

Urban Redevelopment

On the site of a former bus depot, Italian architecture firm Labics has completed a series of buildings on a common pedestal that includes commercial spaces and a public library at ground level, offices on the first floor and public spaces on top of those. Three buildings are perched above this public area – one with more offices and the other two with apartments. The first residential building is a tower containing small and medium-sized flats, partially enclosed by a horizontal glass brise-soleil. The second building contains luxury duplex apartments and is clad in aluminium panels that provide adjustable sun shading and a playful, ever-changing envelope.

Also

Affordable housing in Los Angeles

A profile of Antonin Ziegler

And

An interview with Carlos M. Teixeira, cofounder of studio Vazio